A Bournville Assortment

by

Margaret A. Broomfield

With love and many happy memories.
Auntie Peggy.

William Sessions Limited
The Ebor Press
York England

Peggy Broomfield.

ISBN 1 85072 167 X

*I dedicate this book
to my family and friends,
past, present and future*

Printed in 10 on 11 point Plantin Typeface
by William Sessions Limited
The Ebor Press, York England

Acknowledgements

I ACKNOWLEDGE WITH SINCERE THANKS the following for their permission to quote from copyright and other sources:

Sir Adrian Cadbury, for quotations from Richenda Scott's *Elizabeth Cadbury 1858-1951*, published by George G. Harrap and Co. Ltd.

Cadbury Ltd., Bournville, for extracts from their publication, *An Unemployment Relief Scheme 1933*.

Professor Gordon Cherry, Chairman, Bournville Village Trust, for extracts from Bournville Village Trust publications.

Constable and Co. Ltd., for quotations from Iolo A. Williams' *The Firm of Cadbury*.

Mr Bill Rice, Chairman, Bournville Village Council, for extracts from sundry Bournville Year Books and other Bournville Village Council publications.

Mr Nigel Hastilow, Editor, *The Birmingham Post*, for quotes from his Environment Correspondent Mr Ian McTear's report on *The High Court Action 1991*.

Simon and Schuster, Inc., New York, for quotations from A. G. Gardiner's *The Life of George Cadbury*.

I am also indebted to Mr Andrew MacFarlane, Headmaster of Bournville Junior School and Mr Ray Aldington, of Kings Norton, for allowing me to use in full the article entitled *The Carillon*, to be found in the booklet *Bournville Junior School, the First Eighty Years 1906-1986*, published in 1986.

I thank Mr John Bartlett and Mrs Margaret Glen for allowing me to use quotes from their publication *An Account of Weoley Hill United Reformed Church 1915-1983*.

Thanks are also due to Mr L. H. Pankhurst of Weoley Hill, who provided much of the information for the item on Weoley Hill.

My thanks also to Mr G. M. Davies for allowing me to use his article entitled *The Christmas Tree on the Green*, originally published in *The Carillon* (Bournville Village News), Spring 1993, and to Mr K. A. Newman for permission to use his article, *Froggatt's Farm*, Carillon, Autumn 1991.

I wish to thank Mr John A. Lewis of Lickey, and Mrs Rita Wallace, of Bournville, for their contribution with regard to *Bournville Model Yacht Club*, and *Development in the 80's*, respectively.

I am indebted to my cousins, Robert and Gordon Slater, for allowing me to use the photograph of their grandfather's Foden lorry; to Mr Leslie H. Pankhurst for supplying the photographs of Green Meadow Road, 1930's and Weoley Hill Estate Office. My thanks also to Mr Stanley Crook for lending me the photographs of Bournville Village Steam Laundry and to Miss Audrey Langston for making available the photographs of the Woodlands Hospital. I thank Miss Pamela Moffat for the picture of Yew Tree Farm and Mr John A. Lewis for the photograph of the Yachting Pool.

I thank Professor Gordon Cherry, Chairman Bournville Village Trustees and Mr Bill Rice, Chairman Bournville Village Council, for allowing me to use photographs from various Bournville publications.

I am grateful to Mr Reg Harris for the time he spent photographing some of the more recent buildings of Bournville Estate.

I wish to thank all those who encouraged me to pursue my project in the early days of my endeavours, together with those who, by giving financial support, have made the publication of *A Bournville Assortment* possible. My sincere thanks to them all.

Finally, Mrs Kate Wallbank must be afforded special mention, for it was she who spent many hours diligently reading through and correcting my original manuscript. Her friendly constructive criticism proved to be invaluable and I am greatly indebted to her.

Foreword

by Sir Adrian Cadbury

I WAS GLAD TO ACCEPT Margaret Broomfield's invitation to contribute a Foreword to her book, because of the interest which we share in the history of Bournville and because our recollections of the Village and of the Bournville Works cover the same period.

A Bournville Assortment will prove an invaluable source of reference to anyone who wishes to understand how Bournville grew from its modest beginnings a century ago to the town within a city which it has become today. Margaret Broomfield traces with care the various steps in the development of the Estate and identifies when the separate groups of houses which make up present-day Bournville were built and the purpose which lay behind their construction.

The record of how the original 143 houses grew to meet the needs of increasingly varied groups of residents is brought to life by the social detail against which Margaret Broomfield sets the housing scene. For the early years her sources are, as she tells us, the books and artefacts on Bournville which she has collected during her life. I find it fascinating, for example, that in the early 1900's mowing machines could be hired at 2d. an hour and books upon gardening borrowed 'at the uniform rate of a half penny a week from Mr Dawes, Arley House, Linden Road'.

From there on the historical back ground becomes more personal as she builds the story of Bournville round that of her family. The family link started with her grandfather's move to Selly Oak Road in 1908, when he was working in the Bournville Cocoa Block, and it continues to this day. The development of the Estate is thus seen through the eyes of a family which lived through two World Wars, the depression of the 1930's and the changing social attitudes of more recent times. What the book conveys is a feel for what it was like like to live on the Estate and to be part of the Bournville community during the last hundred years.

Two characteristics of Bournville which differentiate it, I suspect, from most other housing developments of its size are well brought out by the author. The first is the degree to which, from George Cadbury onwards, the Trust has wished the governance of Bournville to be in the hands of those that lived there. Evidence for this are the early co-partnership housing schemes and the way in which the Trust provided facilities for leisure and recreation but entrusted their management to those who used them.

The second feature of Bournville, which to certain extent follows on from the first, is that it is a joint creation of the Trust and of those who have lived and are living on the Estate. The Trust provided the framework for development and set the standards of design, layout and upkeep which are the hallmark of Bournville. It did not, however, impose on the community a centrally determined development plan. Bournville has grown organically through a collection of separate initiatives, aimed at meeting particular needs. It is those who have built their houses on the Estate and those who have lived there who have given Bournville its special character.

I remain grateful to Margaret Broomfield for bringing together so much interesting and useful information about the development of Bournville and for providing for posterity a personal and family record of its first hundred years.

Adrian Cadbury .

30th July, 1995

Contents

Introduction

FOR MANY YEARS NOW my family and friends, knowing that I have many books and artefacts relating to Bournville, have encouraged me to write an account of the Village, its birth, early life and growth, and the development of adjacent land which has resulted in the Bournville Estate as we view it today. At the same time I have tried to interweave items which relate to the ways in which members of my family have lived in and been a part of the area.

I am an inveterate 'magpie' and as a result have many photographs and mementoes which I hope will help to present an informative account of Bournville from its beginnings to the present day.

Bournville itself has never been a 'Company' village attached to the Cadbury factory. However, I feel strongly that with the fairly recent opening of 'CADBURY WORLD', and the subsequent upsurge of visitors to the neighbourhood, it is opportune for such people to be given the chance to learn a little of and see for themselves how George Cadbury's dream was put into practice at the beginning of this century.

I have been fortunate in having lived in Bournville all my life and have had the privilege to know many of the people mentioned in the narrative. Memories of some are less clear than others, but they all have played a part in my life and I am grateful for having traversed life's path with them.

Location of Bournville

Bournville is built on land which was originally part of the ancient Manor of Northfield and Weoley. When, in 1878, Richard and George Cadbury decided to move their expanding business from the centre of Birmingham they bought a site roughly four miles away lying between Selly Oak to the north, Kings Norton to the south and Stirchley to the east. The area was mainly meadow land with the Bourn stream meandering its way from west to east. Any already existing buildings at the time were either farms, large dwelling houses or one or two rows of terraced houses. Ordnance survey maps of the time show dwellings with names such as White Hill House, Griffins Brook House, Bournbrook House, The Davids, Belmont, Woodbrooke, Rokesley, New House Farm, The Dell.

A geological survey was made by Professor W. S. Bolton of Birmingham University in the early 1920's and the following results were established.

The highest points of the Estate are nearing six hundred feet above sea level and the few little brooks and streams which flow through the fields find their way into the River Tame, which in turn joins the River Trent, and finally finds an outlet to the sea by way of the River Humber on the East Coast.

The Birmingham fault passes through the Estate; on the west side of it there is generally speaking, sand, gravel, Keuper sandstone, and on the east side, with the exception of a few glacial drifts of sand, practically nothing but Keuper marl.

In 1881 Woodbrooke became the home of George Cadbury and his wife Mary (nee Tylor). They had married in 1873 and at the time of the move had two sons, Edward and George. There were to be three more children of the marriage; Henry Tylor, Isabel and Eleanor. Mr A. G. Gardiner's *Life of George Cadbury*, written in 1923, tell us that

the house was a substantial and commodious dwelling, standing in the midst of large well-wooded grounds, well beyond the then limits of Birmingham, and on the great road to Bristol. Off this road to the left, and about a mile from Woodbrooke, was the firm's factory. The house was thus convenient alike for the needs of his business, and for those of his increasing family. It was here that, in 1887, he suffered the heaviest bereavement that had befallen him in the death of the wife, to whom he was deeply attached.

George Cadbury married his second wife, Elizabeth Mary Taylor in 1888 and again we learn from Mr Gardiner's account

the union was in every respect a happy one, and of it were born six children, Laurence, Norman, Dorothea, Egbert, Mollie and Ursula.

The family were to move to The Manor House, Northfield (previously known as New House Farm, and described as a mansion with a coach-house), in 1894, and that was to remain the family home until the death of Dame Elizabeth Cadbury in 1951.

The Birmingham News published a supplement on 28th October 1922 entitled 'Mr George Cadbury, Special Memoir' and from it we learn a little more about Woodbrooke. It states,

> George Cadbury was pondering over the best use to which he could put his former house when he learned that the Society of Friends were casting about for some permanent settlement where social and religious studies could be pursued.

> Therefore in 1903 he made over Woodbrooke to Trustees in order that it might be put to this purpose. The building stood in eleven acres of grounds laid out as flower, fruit and vegetable gardens, with shrubberies, walks, croquet lawns, tennis courts and a charming lake.

Thus it was that Woodbrooke became the foundation of what was to become the Selly Oak Colleges, with Kingsmead, Westhill, Fircroft and Carey Hall following on fairly quickly.

In recent years the grounds of Woodbrooke have been scheduled as a site of importance for Nature Conservation.

Early Development

The building of the Cadbury Factory had begun in 1879 and was undertaken by men directly employed by brothers, Richard and George Cadbury. Work was supervised by a foreman bricklayer on loan from the engineering firm of Messrs Tangye. The brothers took great interest in the development of their plans and on occasions would transport senior staff from the Birmingham city centre Bridge Street works for them to see for themselves the progress being made. It wasn't until 1895 that the brothers negotiated for and bought the Bournbrook Hall Estate comprising 140 acres and adjacent to the factory. This was the land on which the Bournville Village was to be built. A pamphlet giving objects of the undertaking states:

1. To make it easy for working men to own houses with large gardens secure from the danger of being spoilt either by the building of factories or by interference with the enjoyment of sun, light, and air.

2. The Bournville Estate consists of about 140 acres of land, prettily situated, and easily accessible from Selly Oak, Stirchley, and Bournville, on the west side of the West Suburban Railway, within five minutes' walk of Bournville, and within about fifteen minutes' walk of Selly Oak Station.

3. The land will be let upon a lease for 999 years, subject to a ground rent varying according to situation of the plot of between ½d. and 1d. per yard.

4. An out and out sale at cost price would have been preferred to a long lease, but the latter is necessary, in order that, for the benefit of all, the conditions for maintaining the rural appearance of the district and the comfort of the inhabitants may be enforced.

5. None of the houses must be below a given size, or cost more than £150; this will secure a superior class of quiet and respectable tenants. Only a certain amount of building will be allowed on each plot, so there will be no danger of gardens being overshadowed and spoiled, or that the neighbourhood will lose its pleasant rural aspect, the speculator will not find a footing, as no person will be allowed to build more than four houses. Should the development of the Estate warrant it, the proprietor intends giving a piece of land of about 7 acres for a recreation ground for the use of tenants of the Estate; and two or three small plots as playgrounds for the children; also land for the erection of schools, baths, and Institute, all ultimately being placed under the care of a committee appointed by the tenants.

   All plans for building must be approved by the architect to the Estate.

6. The Estate to be residential only with the exception of retail shops allowed in certain places for the convenience of the inhabitants, otherwise no manufactory, retail shop, or business of any kind permitted, except in connection with the building of houses on the Estate.

7. Mr Cadbury's solicitors will be prepared to find up to £20,000 on mortgage at the rate of 2½% to those who build houses on the Estate and are prepared to pay down one half of the cost, and at 3% to those who can only pay down a

smaller proportion, in the latter case Mr Cadbury will erect the house and take a preparatory agreement for Lease and Mortgage.

Suppose for example a house cost £150 and £30 is paid towards it. The ground rent and interest should be more than covered by the produce of the large garden, especially if poultry should be kept. The interest on £120 at 3% is 72/- per annum or 1/4½d. per week, this is reduced about 1½d. per week per annum if £10 a year is paid towards the principal advanced. The tenants are safe, as in case of death within 10 years from the date of the mortgage Mr Cadbury will be willing to take over the deceased tenant's property and pay the cost price of the same at short notice, provided that the tenant has duly performed the covenants and conditions of the lease and mortgage.

When value of garden is taken into account a man thus at once lives rent free in a house which at the end of about 13 years is his own, subject to the small ground rent, provided he keeps up the annual payment towards discharge of his mortgage. Further particulars can be obtained from Sydney J. Porter, Solicitor, 26 Waterloo Street, Birmingham, or at the Estate Office, near Bournville Station, any day from 9 a.m. to 5 p.m. or Tuesday and Wednesday from 9 a.m. to 8 p.m.

For example.

	£.	s.	d.
Payment in advance	30	0	0
12 yearly payments	120	0	0
Interest diminishing yearly for 12 years	23	8	0
Total payments	173	8	0
12 years' rent of house at 6/- per week	187	4	0

A tenant renting the house pays £13 more and not a brick of the house becomes his own, while by purchase he lives in it rent free, saves money (£13) during the time, and in the end owns a house worth probably more than the £150, the produce of garden more than covering the small ground rent.

The above particulars were also printed in *The Councillor*, on May 29th 1896, where we learn that Mr Wilson Sturge was Mr Cadbury's Estate Agent.

Formation of Bournville Village Trust

In 1900 George Cadbury made it known that he did not wish to be a landlord and so, by placing in their charge 330 acres of land and 313 houses, valued at £172,000 he nominated 12 members of his family to be Trustees.

The Trust Deed is dated 14th December 1900

I have in my possession a booklet *The Bournville Village Trust*, dated 1901. The opening paragraph reads:

In the Deed by which the Bournville Village Trust is created, the Founder, Mr George Cadbury, has clearly set forth the object he had in view. It is there stated that;

The Founder is desirous of alleviating the evils which arise from the insanitary and insufficient accommodation supplied to large numbers of the working classes, and of securing to workers in factories some of the advantages of outdoor village life, with opportunities for the natural and healthful occupation of cultivating the soil. The object is declared to be the amelioration of the condition of the working class and labouring population in and around Birmingham, and elsewhere in Great Britain, by the provision of improved dwellings, with gardens and open spaces to be enjoyed therewith.

The then Secretary to the Trust, John H. Barlow, continues to write thus:

Briefly stated, the steps by which the Founder was led to recognise the necessity for some such scheme are as follows. The overcrowding in the poor insanitary districts of our large cities results, inevitably, in serious moral and physical deterioration.

Shut up in dirty, evil-smelling streets and courts, deprived of fresh air and sunshine, strangers to the sight of grass and flowers and trees, without means of healthy recreation, familiarised with evil from early childhood, and surrounded by vice and temptation on every hand; what wonder if, while some bravely battle against and rise superior to their surroundings, an immense number are broken down by them and go to swell the terrible mass of vicious criminal and diseased humanity which is a disgrace and menace to our country!

Both the character and the physique of our population suffers, and it becomes increasingly manifest that if we are to hold our own in the rivalry of Nations it is imperative that a remedy be found. These facts are, of course, open to all, but they were specially impressed on the mind of the Founder through his association with the working men of Birmingham. For more than forty years he has been Teacher of a men's Bible Class, going into Birmingham every Sunday morning for this purpose. In this way he has learned to know the life histories, and struggles of hundreds of men, and in the efforts to help them to a better life has again and again encountered the barriers caused by their surroundings. He set himself resolutely to face this difficulty, and the most hopeful solution that presented itself, was to give an opportunity for the people to remove from the squalor and temptations of the city and settle amid the wholesome helpful sights and sounds of country life. In a word, the people must be brought 'back to the land'.

Bournville Village was the result of George Cadbury having reached this conclusion, in fact it is reported he once remarked,

If I had not been brought into contact with the people in my Adult Class in Birmingham, and found from visiting the poor how difficult it was to lead a good life in a back street, I should probably never had built Bournville Village. (Ref. *The Birmingham News* Supplement 28.10.1922.)

For the first 10 years after the founding of the Trust all net income was added to the Trust Fund and was available for further development of the Estate. After that sums were put each year to a 'Trustees' Special Expenditure' account, and devoted to such purposes as the endowment of a Lectureship in Town Planning at Birmingham University. Considerable sums were, and continue to be, spent on

Children's Playground, Laurel Grove – Linden Road houses in the background.

research into matters allied to housing and town planning. Although the first Trustees appointed were all members of the Cadbury family, provision was made for the later representation of the City of Birmingham, the University of Birmingham, and The Religious Society of Friends (Quakers), George Cadbury being a birthright member of the latter.

First Housing

News of the experimental village was to spread far and wide and conferences and lectures on Bournville were arranged, and visitors from far and near were made welcome. According to *The Birmingham News* supplement, 28th October 1922,

> The influence of Bournville Village has spread far beyond Birmingham. Visitors to it from all parts of the world have taken away with them an enthusiasm for the ideals for which it stands, and today there are garden villages of this kind in practically every civilised country.

The first people to come and live in Bournville were from varying backgrounds. Some were already employees, others were acquaintances of George Cadbury, men he had met through his work for the

Shops – corner of Maryvale and Linden Roads.

Adult School movement, and there were others who were fortunate enough to be rehoused from the slums of the city centre.

Early Bournville publications tell us the first houses to be built after the founding of the Village Trust had the following accommodation:

Ground floor.	Living-room or kitchen	16ft. 6ins. x 11ft. 6ins.
	Parlour	13ft. 6ins. x 11ft. with bay
	Scullery	7ft. 6ins. x 7ft. 6 ins.
	Lobby / Larder	
First floor.	Bedroom 1.	13ft. 6ins. x 11ft.
	Bedroom 2.	11ft. 6ins. x 9ft.
	Bedroom 3.	7ft. 3ins. x 8ft. 6 ins.
	Linen closet.	

There was also a bath in the kitchen, and the usual outhouses.

The larger cottages had similar accommodation but the rooms were bigger and an extra bedroom took the place of the linen closet.

In the largest houses, bathrooms, with hot and cold water were provided.

The Village was served by Birmingham City with gas, water and sewers; the rates, including water, amounted to 5/3d. in the £. Rents from 6/6d. per week (rates included), to 9/-d. per week (rates not included).

9

Sycamore Road looking towards the Village Green.

Houses in Sycamore Road showing the variety in design.

Further examples of variety in design. (Sycamore Road.)

Beech Road running down to the Park with Thorn Road in the background.

House at the corner of Bournville Lane and Beech Road.

Hay Green Lane – the gate marks the point where present day Cedar Road joins Hay Green Lane.

Houses at the southern end of Selly Oak Road.

Linden Road – east side.

Linden Road – west side.

12

The houses were semi-detached or in blocks of four, and monotony was avoided by the introduction of a great variety of design.

The buildings were designed by the then Bournville Trust architect Mr W. Alexander Harvey. He was to leave the Trust in 1902 but remained as their consulting architect for many years.

The average garden space allotted to each house was in the region of 600 square yard. Plum, apple and pear trees were planted at the end of each garden and these, besides yielding a good supply of fruit, formed a pleasant screen for the backs of the houses. It was estimated that under spade cultivation gardens of these dimensions would yield a return of from 2/-d. to 2/6d. a week in fruit and vegetables.

Items of General Interest

The Bournville Village Council Annual Report for 1904 tells us the Annual Outing for that year took place on June 18th, the venue being Ragley Hall, by kind permission of the Marquis of Hertford.

The same year the Children's Festival was

favoured with brilliant summer weather, and was, throughout, a day of unalloyed joy, whilst the large amount of work involved was forgotten in the general pleasure given.

Under the heading 'Open-air Concerts' is written,

the series held this year was an unqualified success, and, owing to this, the Council was encouraged to arrange a programme of 'Winter Entertainments' which included concerts, social evenings, lectures, etc.

The Bath House, situated in Laurel Grove adjacent to the Children's Playground, had been built in about 1897 and was open daily from 9 a.m. to 9 p.m. with the charge for a hot or cold bath being 3d. This charge included the hire of one towel, but soap was ½d. extra!!

In case of Fire, ladders were kept at the Bath House, and Mr B. Cook's, 27 Laburnum Road. There was a Fire Alarm Box at the south end of Willow Road. In subsequent years, others were placed in Woodbrooke Road at the junction with Oak Tree Lane, at the corner of Linden Road and Maryvale Road, and at the junction of Woodlands Park Road and Hay Green Lane. (Very few folk had telephones in their homes in those days and 999 calls were a thing of the future.)

By 1913 there were GPO Post boxes situated at Maryvale Road, Willow Road, Bournville Lane (near the Railway station), Linden Road (north end), and the Post Office. All were cleared six or seven times a day starting between 7.25 a.m. and 8.15 a.m., with the last collection between 7.45 p.m. and 9 p.m., depending on location.

By 1914 Villagers were reminded that in case of accident a member of the St John Ambulance Association resided at the following addresses.

Mr J. Parrish	4 Bournville Cottages.
Mr R. Fowler	8 Elm Road.
Mr T. Kendall	10 Holly Grove.
Mr A. Lea	31 Willow Road.
Mr A. Morris	40 Raddle Barn Lane.
Mr A. Beard	6 Willow Road.
Mr W. Whitcombe	Woodbrooke Road.
Mr H. Smith	107 Bournville Lane.
Miss G. Wright	94 Linden Road.
Miss A. Wride	14 Laburnum Road.
Mr G. Beale	59 Selly Oak Road.

The Bath House, Bournville.

Bournville's first Post Office, 84 Linden Road.

Gardeners' Association

The 1905 Annual Report of the Bournville Village Council gives details of 'The Gardeners' Association'. We read:

> Bournville is called the Garden Village, and one of the chief objects of its Founder is to make it possible for people to realise and appreciate the pleasure and healthfulness of gardening.

Three shows of produce were held each year, the Rose Show in July, Flower Show in late August and an Autumn show.

In 1900 there had been 1,000 entries from the Village, an indication of the interest taken in gardening at the time. In addition to cultivation of their plot, many residents kept poultry, the produce of which helped to supplement the family fare in the larder. Some folk were making a profit from bee-keeping.

The printed balance sheets give us the following information:

> Bournville Village Council records £33. 0s. 0d. in the bank and 8/9½d. in Treasurer's hand
> Village Flower Show a balance of.................. £11. 9s 10d.
> The Open-Air Concerts had a balance of .... £3. 18s. 11½d.

15

Gardeners' Association made a profit of .... £1. 2s. 1½d.
Bournville Tenants' Annual Party a balance of .... 2d.

Prizes awarded at the various shows ranged from 1/-d. to £1. 0s. 0d. Garden tools could be had on hire from the Bath House in Laurel Grove, or from Mr B. Cook, 27 Laburnum Road. He was a rent collector. The amounts charged for the hire of tools were as follows:

Mowing machine .... 2d. per hour.
Roller .... 1d. per hour.
Shears .... 1d. per hour.
Long-handled shears .... 1d. per hour.
Edging shears .... 1d. per hour.
Long ladder .... 1d. per hour.
Short ladder .... 1d. per hour.
Edging knife .... 1d. per hour.
Scythe .... 1d. per hour.
Wheelbarrow .... 1d. per hour.
Fruit drying apparatus .... 3d. per day.

Books upon gardening subjects could be obtained at the uniform charge of a half-penny per week from Mr Dawes, Arley House, Linden Road.

By 1916 the Gardeners' Association reported it had made continued progress and 1915 had been the most successful year it had ever had. It would appear there were between 250 and 300 members. Two hundred and forty gardens were judged and the following crops were grown.

135 members grew beet, 146 grew broad beans,
214 runner beans, 162 cabbage, 155 cauliflower,
92 celery, 103 carrots, 74 cucumber,
240 flowers, 239 fruit, 205 herbs, 76 leeks,
158 marrows, 148 onions, 166 peas, 163 parsnips,
204 potatoes, 103 shallots, 115 turnips.

The report goes on to say these figures perhaps convey only a vague idea of the crops grown and the value of these crops to the tenant. (We must remember all this was happening at the time of the First World War and any produce would have been more than acceptable.)

One member who grew potatoes on a 50 square yard plot obtained 310 lbs. as a result. The seed cost 3/-d. the probable cost of manure about 1/-d. (I am reliably informed the cost of seed today for a similar

16

sized plot might be between £12–£15 with manure or fertiliser costing £30 and the yield could well be in the region of 480 lbs). Members paid 1/-d. subscription each year and on presenting their membership card were able to receive 10% off seeds and 5% off plants and bulbs when purchasing from the Village Nursery.

Shops

By 1908 the shops on the Village Green had been built and the annual reports of The Bournville Village Council (formed in 1900) include advertisements for;

Daniel Roy, High class plain and fancy bread baker.

James Underwood, draper, hosier and haberdasher.

O. W. Evans, Bournville Pharmacy.

J. A. Shipley, family grocer and provision merchant.

Thos. E. Lowe, Estate butcher.

Bryden and Son, village tailors and outfitters.

John T. Payne, English and foreign fruiter and greengrocer, fish and poultry salesman.

M. J. Patteson, The Post Office.
(Bournville's first post office was at house no. 84 Linden Road.)

F. Davies, china and hardware stores.

Lloyds Bank, manager: A. H. Harris.

These retail outlets were additional to the already existing shops found situated within the Bournville boundary. For instance those in Raddle Barn Lane (later to become Raddlebarn Road).

F. Wagstaff, practical boot and shoe maker and repairer.

Gittins's, ironmongers, corn and seed merchants.

On the southern edge of the Village there were;

H. W. Smith, grocery, provisions, game, dairy and farm produce.

James Healey, boot maker and repairer.

W. Sanders, confectioner and caterer.

Alfred Allely, ironmonger.

Other advertisements tell us of Ye Old Farm Inn, with J. Bodycote proprietor.

Hot joints daily.

Cyclists and Parties catered for.

Mineral waters and refreshments at popular prices.

Horses taken in to bait.

Cigars and tobacco.

Laurence Holding, builder, shopfitter and general craftsmen in wood was living at 10 Thorn Road. He offered;

Estimates free. Special lines in Greenhouses, garden frames etc.

Mr Frank Austin's Band (formed in 1897) could be hired for;

'Balls, Conversaziones, Soirees, Concerts and Dramatic performances'. Only EXPERIENCED MUSICIANS engaged.

Mr Austin resided at 17 Beech Road.

By 1913 H. J. Moore (who had been with J. W. Lill and Sons, Bristol Street, for 17 years), was advertising as *Upholsterer*.

Suites re-stuffed and re-covered in any material.

Wool and hair mattresses re-made and re-ticked.

All kinds of Upholstery repairs.

Mr Moore lived at 50 Beech Road.

A. L. Wadley of 41 Beech Road and H. J. Wride of 16 Laburnum Road were painters and decorators.

Mr William Sheward, dairyman and general haulier, ran Hay Green Farm.

By 1917 a Mr William Beck, a practical watch and clock maker with 30 years' experience was advertising his skills from 73 Linden Road. In 1920, no. 59 Linden Road was used by Foreign Mission Industries. Was this a forerunner of the Mission Industries shop that I recall, from days of my youth, being at the Bristol Road end of College Walk?

By 1923 Bournville Village Steam Laundry had opened in the Sandpits, Acacia Road. The proprietor was a Mr Crook, and his son, Mr Stanley Crook of Bryony Road, Selly Oak, tells me his father and an aunt began the business in two cottages situated in Oak Tree Lane in about 1902.

The cottages were demolished in the 1960's to make way for the present Oak Tree House. In 1924 Field and Pearson and Hole and Son also had premises at the Sandpits. They were joiners. W. Slater and Son were haulage contractors and were at 38 Selly Oak Road. At Five Gates, Willow Road, the site of the Estate builder's yard, there were premises referred to as The Handicrafts, and Mr H. Brown Morrison, Silversmith, carried on his craft there.

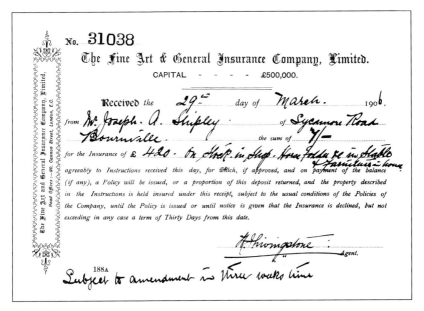

Growth of the Estate in the Early Years

The Estate grew, during the first 25 years of this century, due to pockets of land being leased by the Bournville Trust to various housing societies. The Trustees wished to demonstrate a possible method by which ownership of land and control of planning could be vested in the municipality, while at the same time the responsibility for development, design, selection of tenants, maintenance, repairs and the whole business of management, was placed in the hands of a co-partnership housing society to which all tenants would belong. The first such group, formed in 1906, was entitled <u>BOURNVILLE TENANTS LIMITED</u>. The Trustees leased 20 acres of the Estate to them with a promise of more if required. By 1911 there were 261 members and 145 houses had been built. No. 216 Northfield Road was used as Bournville Tenants' Estate Office. This development can be seen to the

*Haulage contractor
W. Slater with his son
William.*

*The Laundry before
the introduction of
motorised vehicles.*

*The staff – Bournville
Village Laundry.*

*Bournville Village
Steam Laundry,
Acacia Road.*

*Shops – Bournville
Village Green – early
30's.*

south west of Bournville in the area bounded by the southern end of Woodlands Park Road, Northfield Road, Hawthorne Road and Kingsley Road.

WEOLEY HILL LIMITED was formed in 1914 with the object of developing land to the north west of the main Bristol Road. Nearly 500 houses were built and sold on 99-year leases. Many of the properties were built to individual purchaser's requirements and the estate fast developed into a very attractive area of Birmingham.

Weoley Hill has its own parkway with bowling green, tennis courts, and cricket pitch/football field. It also has a village hall which is used each week day by a local playgroup. In addition jumble sales, art and craft sales and other local functions take place there. (My parents gave me my 21st birthday celebrations there in the spring of 1949.)

BOURNVILLE WORKS HOUSING SOCIETY LIMITED was set up in 1919 to meet the demand for houses from employees of Cadbury Brothers. This was financed by the firm, who advanced money through their Pension Fund, which, in turn, benefited from the interest and repayment of capital. The Society leased 50 acres and let over 360 houses to its shareholders. The dwellings are two-or-three bedroom type with a few having four bedrooms. As at Weoley Hill, provision was made for an open space to be preserved at the rear of the Estate and was laid out as a recreational ground. This was one of the few portions of the Estate which was reserved for Cadbury Bros. employees. The development can be seen in parts of Hay Green Lane, Woodlands Park Road and Mulberry Road to the west of Bournville village.

In 1920, thanks to Cadbury Brothers Limited making a grant for the investigation of methods of building other and cheaper than the usual method of brick, the Bournville Trust examined over 40 different types of construction of which five were selected for experiment, and seven dwellings were built. These were a wooden bungalow, a brick bungalow, pise de terre (rammed earth) bungalow and two pairs of concrete houses. The experiment aroused wide interest, attracting several thousand visitors including deputations from municipalities and delegates from the International Housing Congress, representing 21 countries. However, after reviewing the whole question it was decided that no other method was so economical for the district as the, by this time, well tried brick. (Some of these experimental homes can still be seen in Hay Green Lane near its junction with Bournville Lane.)

In 1923 WOODLANDS HOUSING SOCIETY LIMITED built 79 houses with the intention of selling or leasing them to members of the Society, but a number were let on rent. These homes can be seen in Hole Lane and Innage Road.

Also in 1923 RESIDENTIAL FLATS LIMITED built St George's Court, a block of self-contained flats and bed-sitting rooms, with a common dining room, at the corner of Oak Tree Lane and Woodbrooke Road, Bournville. They were let to professional and business women.

Another development taking place on the Estate in 1924 was the building of bungalows by Cadbury Brothers for single women in their employ. These dwellings can be seen in Cedar Road and Cedar Close.

Further such bungalows were built in Griffins Brook Lane and Griffins Brook Close in 1928.

In 1925 an experimental pair of 'Telford' steel houses were erected at the corner of Cedar Road and Hay Green Lane (now the site of a two storey block of flats), with the following accommodation:

Living room	14ft. 1½ins. x 17ft. 3ins.
Scullery	8ft. 5½ins. x 10ft. 7½ins.
Bathroom, larder, coals and lavatory adjoining scullery.	
Bedrooms	10ft. 8in. x 17ft. 3ins.
	10ft. 8in. x 8ft. 2ins.
	8ft. 11in. x 14ft. 2ins.

The contract price was £465 for each house, erected, exclusive of drains, foundations, and garden paths, which cost £110 more, nothing being included for garden work.

I seem to recall these homes were always considered damp and condensation ran down the windows, so I can only presume that that is why they were demolished to make way for the present day block of flats.

During the late 1930's land to the south west of the Estate was made available for the building of individual homes and a few retail outlets, by private builders, which resulted in the development of the Heath Road shopping area and the Claines Road, Somerdale Road, Knighton Road, and Newent Road. At the same time homes were being built in Meadowbrook Road to the west of the Estate.

This then was how the Estate grew from its inception in 1895 to the outbreak of war in 1939.

Roads, Trees and Open Spaces

ROADS

All roads on Bournville were planned with regard for the contours of the land, which is undulating.

When the village was founded unnecessary expense was caused by the excessive width of carriageway required by bye-laws, even in side

*Kingsley Road –
Bournville Tenants'
Limited.*

*Northfield Road –
Bournville Tenants'
Limited.*

*Woodlands Park Road
– Bournville Tenants'
Limited.*

Witherford Way –
Bristol Road – Weoley
Hill Limited.

Tennis Courts –
Weoley Hill.
Junction of
Weoley Hill – Fox Hill
in the background.

Fox Hill looking
towards Witherford
Way – Weoley Hill
Limited.

25

Junction of Weoley Hill – Fox Hill.

Weoley Hill – circa 1919.

Weoley Hill – circa 1929.

26

*Hay Green Lane.
Bournville Works
Housing Society
Limited.*

*Bournville Works
Housing Society
Limited, corner of
Hay Green Lane and
Mulberry Road.*

*Griffins Brook Lane
– 'sunshine homes',
principal rooms facing
south.*

Mulberry Road.

Start of a day's outing?
Blackthorn Road –
Mulberry Road.

Experimental houses –
Hay Green Lane.

Woodlands Housing Society Limited.

Bungalows built by Cadbury Brothers for single women in their employ.

*St George's Court.
Built by Residential
Flats Limited.*

*Green Meadow Road,
Nos. 36–46. Weoley
Hill – final phase of
building prior to the
2nd World War.*

roads. These requirements were soon relaxed and by the 1920's the usual Estate roads, where no through traffic was expected, had a carriageway 18ft. wide. This was the minimum width allowed except in short culs-de-sac. The most important roads were wider and had deeper building lines. Bournville roads were usually flanked by grass verges six feet wide and by footpaths the same width. Trees were planted in the grass verges where practicable.

The normal distance from house-front to house-front was 82ft.

A road-making department was maintained by the Village Trust for some years before responsibility was handed over to Birmingham City Council.

TREES

Many species of tree can be found on the Estate from Whitebeam, Crimson and Cockspur thorn, Japanese crab, Hizahura cherry, Acer Negunda, Almond, Mountain ash, Silver birch, to Pyrus sorbus, Laburnum, and Amanogoura cherry.

In addition to the trees that line the roadsides, ornamental plantations which were designed to produce effects of blossom and autumn colouring, can be found at various points of the Estate. They include varieties already mentioned, and maples of various types and horse-chestnuts have been added.

In one or two instances, plantations of oak and beech have been made, with larch, spruce and scots fir to act as nurses.

The trees on the Estate were cared for by Bournville Village Trust forestry department, under the control of a trained forester. Where possible, existing forest trees were left standing at the roadside, and in gardens. I had one such in my garden. It was an oak and had been hollow for many years. Children delighted in climbing up steps to a height of about seven feet and then entering the trunk of the tree to emerge at the foot a few seconds later. Unfortunately, a few years ago it had to be felled. The tree surgeons who cut it down for me reckoned it was nigh on 200 years old. It was one of a row that had clearly been a part of a hedgerow. Others can be seen in gardens on either side of mine.

OPEN SPACES

Roads and open spaces were further beautified by the planting of crocus and daffodil bulbs and other spring flowers in grass verges, and other convenient plots of grass. Bournville Village Green and the central reservation of Weoley Hill really do provide a wonderful show in spring-time, and the ornamental cherry trees that line parts of Woodbrooke Road and Bournville Lane, adjacent to the Yachting Pool, are spectacular in the middle weeks of May.

I understand such planting of bulbs, as for example those in Weoley Hill, was instigated by individual residents, in that case by Mrs W. O. Duncan, who paid for crocuses and daffodil bulbs to be set. This shows how the impulse to beautify spread from the Founder to the residents.

Proof positive of the Trust's aims to enhance the area for which they are responsible can be found in the Bournville Estate Residents' Handbook for 1970.

In the landscaping of the Estate the Trustees have paid particular attention to the proper treatment of the Bristol Road. It is one of the most important roads into the city and they have done their best to see that the effect created by the belts of tall trees on either side of the road is not damaged by unsightly structures. They were therefore most anxious that the new pedestrian bridge from the west side of Bristol Road to the east should have architectural merit. Accordingly they contributed towards the cost of the structure, which was built to higher standards than the city would normally have undertaken. The bridge was opened on the 14th November 1969, by the Chairman of the Trust, Mr L. J. Cadbury.

Camp Wood

Camp Wood, formerly known as Stocks Wood, is situated in Maple Road/Acacia Road. The area is beautiful at all seasons of the year, particularly in the Spring and early Summer when the daffodils, bluebells, wild anemones and other wild flowers of those seasons together with the newly opening buds of the assorted trees, especially the beech trees, provide one with a wonderful vista. The road through the wood used to be open to vehicles during the day-time all the year round, with entrances in Acacia and Maple Roads. However when, in recent years, the bungalows were built in Stocks Wood and the Bournville Garden Centre was modernised, traffic was restricted to pedestrians, or those in cars who were visiting the centre.

In recent years the area has been scheduled as a site of importance for Nature Conservation.

The area was originally the site of Bournville Village Nursery, and was intended solely for the use of local residents. However in the 50's and 60's it was leased to Ten Acres and Stirchley Co-operative Society, and some years later a local young man, Derek Walker, took over the business, and it is as a result of his foresight and hard work together with that of members of his family and employees that we see the thriving Garden Centre of today. Derek had started work in Birmingham Parks Department and his father was, for a time, park-keeper at Woodlands Park.

The Centre offers garden requisites from lawn seed to exotic house plants, walling stone to garden furniture, trellis, garden plants, shrubs, bulbs, seeds, even items for aquatic and wild-life gardens, books on horticultural and botanic subjects. At Christmas time the place is transformed into a wonderful grotto usually depicting an Olde Worlde scene. Folk come from many parts of the Midlands to buy their garden requirements.

Derek's brother, Kenneth, although moving away from Birmingham for a time, now runs a Tree Surgery and Garden Landscaping business in Bournville, together with his son Stephen.

Situated between Camp Wood and Minworth Greaves is a small car park. For many years there stood a sandstone monument on this site. Early records of Bournville tell us it was erected by a Colonel Rann who resided at Bournbrook Hall, the site of which is now occupied by Cadbury/Schweppes Girls' Recreation Ground in Bournville Lane. Colonel Rann built the monument in memory of his favourite charger and it marked the spot where the horse was buried. By 1842, Mr Stocks, from whom we get the name for Stocks Wood, was living at Bournbrook Hall, and as Colonel Rann had previously owned the Estate it is probable the pillar was getting on for 180 years old when the time came for it to be moved or demolished to make way for the present car park a few years ago.

Bournville Park – Part 1

It was in 1906 that definite steps were taken with a view to the land on either side of the Bourn brook being opened as a Park. The Village Trust was then approached on the subject, but while readily agreeing to the space being handed over to a committee of residents as managers, it had no funds that could be used for the upkeep of a Park. The Trustees, however, very generously offered to provide (from private funds) half the cost of maintenance, providing the inhabitants of the Village would make themselves responsible for the other half. On March 13th 1907, a public meeting was held in Ruskin Hall to consider the question. The matter was discussed thoroughly and among the points dealt with was the question of handing the Park over to the local authority. In the end it was decided to retain the Park and place it in the hands of a Management Committee.

The Park was open each week-day from 8 a.m. to sunset and from 10 a.m. to sunset on Sundays, except on the day of the Flower Show.

33

Bournville Park with Junior School in background.

The Park-keeper was a Mr H. Hopper and he lived at 60 Beech Road, next to the Park. It was his job to supervise the upkeep of the flower beds, tennis courts, bowling greens, pathways and all the grassland and shrubbery. He too was responsible for the ringing of the handbell a quarter of an hour before sunset so that folk would not be in the park when the gates were locked for the night. (I well remember this ritual from the days of my childhood, living as I did right opposite the park. The iron gates and railings were dismantled during the Second World War and went to be made into munitions. After the war they were replaced by wooden railings.)

Requisites for Games in the Park were for hire as follows:

Tennis   Fourpence per half-hour for four persons. This is to include the court being marked and the net; the players to find their own rackets and balls. Single sets at the same rate, i.e. fourpence per half-hour. If rackets and balls are provided, the charge to be sixpence per half-hour.

Bowls	Twopence per hour each person, the committee finding the bowls. Three half-pence per hour each person if the player provides his own bowls.
Croquet	Penny per hour each person; all requisites found.
Badminton	Penny each for four persons per hour, or twopence each for two persons per hour; all requisites found.
Lawn-skittles	Penny per person per half-hour.
Football	For boys twopence per hour.

The question whether the Park should be handed over to the local authority was again raised at a Tenants' Annual Gathering in 1914. After lengthy discussion it was decided that a vote be taken of the residents. This resulted as follows:–

> 281 for handing the Park over.
> 45 against.
> 10 were neutral.
> 49 papers returned unsigned.

In addition to sporting activities the park was also used for open-air concerts. In 1906 such concerts

> were again successful; the weather was favourable and the attendance good, but the contributions received were not, unfortunately, quite sufficient to meet the necessary expenses.

My Grandparents

My maternal grandparents and their children were the first members of my family to live in Bournville.

Grandfather had been born in 1868 at Belbroughton, Worcestershire and, like his father and grandfather before him, had been employed by Isaac Nash as a scythegrinder. The industry suffered a decline in the late 1880's and as a result grandfather moved to Birmingham and found work with O. C. Hawkes, cabinet makers.

At the time of his marriage in 1894 he was living at 28 Guest Street and his bride-to-be, Clara Hopkins, lived at 20 Mark Street.

Their first home was at 15 Salisbury Place, Moor Green Lane, Kings Heath, from where they moved to 64 Bond Street, Stirchley,

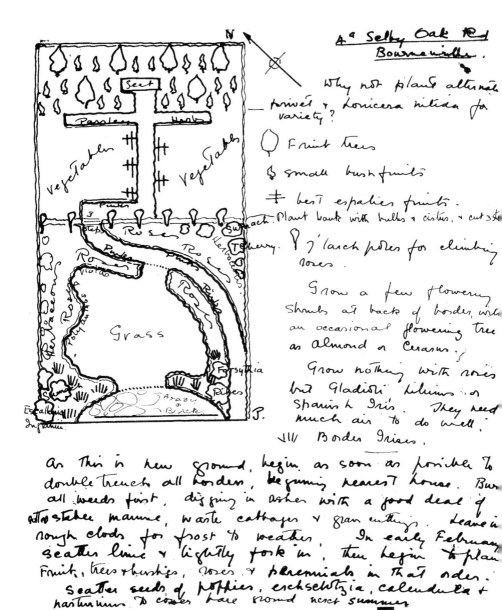

Advice given to my Grandparents with regard to the cultivation of their garden. 1908

thence to 27 Maryvale Road, Stirchley, and finally, in 1908, to 4a Selly Oak Road, Bournville.

By this time grandfather was employed by Cadbury Brothers and was working in the Cocoa Block.

There were five children of the marriage; Charles, Albert, Marian (my mother), Percy and Amy. Sadly, Percy died at the age of two. Charles, Albert and Marian all attended Stirchley School for a time, however, once resident in Bournville, they were enrolled as pupils at the new village school, of which more in a later chapter.

I know very little of those days save that my grandparents and their children were a close-knit loving group, sharing sorrows, joys and concerns of their own and those around them.

At the outbreak of war in 1914 Charles enlisted in the Royal Army Medical Corps. He married in 1916, and from that time onwards his relationship with the family became strained and his visits infrequent. Incredibly he always seemed to know when there was a family crisis, and would telephone or simply arrive on our doorstep as if nothing untoward had happened in the previous several years.

I read in Richard Holding's book, *Down along Temeside*, that Albert was a founder member of the Junior Adult School. I know that after serving as a signaller on HMS Hope during the First World War he went on to qualify as a teacher, with his first post being at Bloomsbury Street School, Birmingham and for many years he was a much respected member of staff at Ilmington Road School, Weoley Castle, until his retirement in the early 1960's.

After leaving school my mother found herself working variously for Robert A. Morris, seed merchant of Bristol Street, Barrow's Restaurant in Corporation Street, and Stirchley Co-operative Society, later to become Ten Acres and Stirchley Co-operative Society.

The tales my mother told of those days of her working life, of the times when at 4p.m. on Christmas Eve someone would walk in to Morriss's and order a holly wreath to be delivered to Witton Cemetery, and mother or one of the other junior assistants would have the task of delivery by tram and a fair good walk too, before returning to Bristol Street in time to tidy the shop before being allowed home for Christmas. No Interflora in those days!

In much the same way we heard accounts of her time at the Co-op. She was employed in the Boot and Shoe Department. In those days

My aunt Amy at school – 3rd row back, 4th to the left.

My mother with other staff, Barrow's Restaurant, 1918. 3rd row back 4th to left.

*My uncle Bert
2nd from left.
Uncle Charles far right.*

*Back row. My father,
grandfather, uncle
Bert. Front row.
Mother, grandmother,
aunt Amy.*

retailers kept their premises open until all hours and many was the
time my mother worked until 9 p.m. on Christmas Eve, only to find
that once the shop closed the Directors would bring their families in to
do their last-minute shopping. Christmas Eve was no different from
any other working day in those times.

I am convinced my mother enjoyed her time at work, so much so
that in later years, when my sister and I were old enough, she would
take us to Morriss's to buy the seed potatoes, peas and beans, cabbage
and lettuce seed for the garden; snowdrop, crocus, daffodil and
hyacinth bulbs for planting in bowls. I recall in my mind's eye the shop
being long and narrow with an equally long counter, behind which
there were stacks of shelves and a host of wooden drawers of varying

sizes. Gas lighting was used for illumination in those days, and this together with the creosoted and stained woodwork gave the place an aroma of its own.

Another thing I remember about trips into town are the visits to Barrow's Stores. Some of the 'girls' mother had worked with during the First World War, were still working there in the late 1940's. How tongues would wag when they got together!

My mother was always fond of music and for many years sang with the Co-operative Mixed Voice Choir and was a regular soloist on occasions. In fact I am proud to record that she was one of the first people in Birmingham to sing *Roses of Picardy* in public. A certain Mr Herbert Davey, still living in Bournville to this day, recalls the time he heard my mother sing that song in the Bournville Junior School Hall in 1917, and he confesses he thought she sang so beautifully, the tears rolled down his cheeks, and they still do today when he relates the tale. I wonder if any other people from that audience 78 years ago recall such memories?

Upon leaving school Amy too was employed by Stirchley Co-op and worked in the Drapery Department until her marriage.

Those times must have been very difficult for many people and I know they were hard times for my grandparents and their growing family. They had been hard pressed to finance Albert's teaching studies, so much so that when my mother was considered suitable for an academic career they had had to admit, reluctantly, that they could not afford such a venture. In later life my mother confessed she would have loved to go to University, but it was not to be.

My Father Arrives in Bournville

In the early 1920's, a young man by the name of Edgar Owen arrived in Bournville from Lee Brockhurst, a small hamlet in Shropshire. He had been born there in 1897, had attended the local village school before enlisting, under-age, in the Royal Field Horse Artillery. He served in India during the First World War and, when demobbed, worked for a time in his home county. Due to the lack of steady employment and a difficult home life he decided to move to Birmingham. He applied for and gained a job with Bournville Village Nursery in Maple Road. He and a friend cycled from Lee Brockhurst to Shrewsbury where they continued the journey by train with their

*My parents leaving church after
their wedding 1924.*

*Father with his chickens in the
garden of 46 Raddlebarn Road.*

cycles in the guard's van. All four duly arrived at New Street station. Father was fortunate in having lodgings arranged for him with a Mrs Parsons of 39 Linden Road, and had had instructions to travel to Bournville from the centre of Birmingham by tramcar to Selly Oak. He would often recall the surprise the two friends had when they were told they could not put their cycles on the tram!

Moving from a small hamlet to the new expanding model village must have been quite a big step for my father to take, but he never regretted it. He always spoke very highly of Mrs Parsons and her family and the warmth of the welcome he received when he crossed their threshold.

Having been a lorry driver in the army meant father was employed as such by the nursery, and was to be seen day by day delivering ashes, sand, gravel and fruit trees, to new housing in the Hay Green Lane and Mulberry Road area. The nursery had been established in 1902 and was originally intended only for the development of the Bournville Estate. Some houses were sold, others rented, and each one had ash or

41

gravel paths laid and a selection of fruit trees planted, together with wooden clothes posts in readiness for the hanging of the weekly wash.

The passing of time has seen the nursery's growth. For a time it was leased to Stirchley Co-op. More recently it has been in private hands and is now referred to as a 'Garden Centre'. Whatever the name and whoever the owners, it has always been an oasis where those who delight in the wonders of God's natural world can relax and plan and purchase horticultural items for their own individual plot, be it large or small.

My parents met not long after father's arrival in Bournville and they were married in 1924. The marriage took place at what was then the church but is now the church hall, for although the Anglican Parish of Bournville was formed in 1915, it wasn't until 1925 that the present church of St Francis, a building in the Byzantine style, was built. The officiating clergyman was the Reverend Creed Meredith, vicar of the parish. The newly weds were to have a week's honeymoon at Clent in Worcestershire.

My parents' first home was a Bournville Trust rented house, no. 46 Raddle Barn Road, and there father was able to keep a few chickens to provide the home with eggs, for in those days residents were allowed to keep poultry. A few years ago I met up with an old school friend of mine whose parents were my parents' first neighbours, and in the course of conversation she told me her mother had always remembered my father for the time he spent every dinner hour endeavouring to retrieve his chickens from neighbouring gardens. Some houses on the Estate also had a pig sty. I remember nos. 3 and 5 Selly Oak Road had such a building.

In 1927 my parents moved to 8 Selly Oak Road, which was to be their home for the next 22 years.

My Life with my Grandparents

I was not born in Bournville, presumably because my mother had chosen to have a Nursing Home delivery, and our General Practitioner, Dr James Brown of Stirchley, favoured the Hazelwell Nursing Home in Vicarage Road, Kings Heath. I was brought into the world, on 19th April 1928, by Nurse Roberts of Selly Park. She and my parents became good friends and remained so for the rest of their lives.

My maternal grandfather,
James Hawthorne Guest.

My maternal grandmother,
Clara Guest.

My first home was 8 Selly Oak Road, and my grandparents lived only three houses away at no. 4a. Thus it was that I spent many happy hours in their company. My grandfather retired early through ill-health and that made it very convenient for me, a first grandchild living so near, to be for ever popping in to see him and grandmother.

My pre-school days were happy ones spent helping my mother in the home and garden, playing with other children who were neighbours, walking across the park to the shops on the village green. Once a week I would accompany grandfather on his walk to Stirchley Public Library where he would sit reading through the previous week's newspapers. *The Birmingham Gazette* was his favourite. Our journey was always prefaced with a drink of Cadbury's cocoa. At such a tender age I was allowed a saucerful and bread dippies, a must before a good walk. No local bus to take us in those days. I remember I had to be at 4a for 10 a.m. and would arrive as Stuart Hibberd was finishing the daily weather forecast on the radio. In later years I was told of the day when I let out an ear-piercing shriek as we entered the Bournville Lane railway and canal bridge. This had been because a steam-roller had entered the bridge from the opposite direction and the noise it made had terrified me.

In 1932 my grandfather suffered a severe stroke which resulted in him being bedridden for the remaining three years of his life. One of my most treasured possessions is a brass bell, the type that used to be seen on every shop counter at one time. It is the one that sat on a little table at my grandfather's bedside all those years go.

My grandmother was a devout church-goer, she truly loved her church and was a stalwart member of the Mothers' Union. She had also been a member of the Suffragette movement and had on one occasion chained herself to the railings outside the Selly Oak Hospital. Her other great interest was the Co-operative Women's Guild and she represented the local branch at many conferences. Her political persuasion was directly opposed to that of my father, but they always managed to agree amicably to differ.

She had a great love of literature, particularly poetry, and was an accomplished writer and speaker. Her subjects ranged from the history and development of Birmingham (I remember her telling me the Town Hall foundations were built on the waste from pearl button manufacturing), to the 'Teaching of Sex Hygiene'. An example of her work can be seen in the *Journal of the Royal Sanitary Institute* Vol. XLI, no.3. (1921) where she writes on the subject from a working mother's point of view.

Her speaking engagements took her away from home rarely, but in September 1919 she must have been to some gathering or other at Weston-Super-Mare because as a result she was given an Oxford edition of the Poems of Tennyson. I have that book and in its leaves there is a letter which reads;

High Street

September 17-19

Dear Mrs Guest

At our executive meeting this afternoon there was a unanimous wish expressed that we should send you a small token of our love and esteem. I was deputed to get you something I thought would suit you and I didn't know of anything better than a book of poems. It is not for the value of the present but whenever you spend half an hour with it you will think of the good wishes that come with it. This is very hurried but I thought you should have it at the first possible moment.

With kind regards

Your sincerely,

A. Andrews.

Hope you got safe home from Weston and that your daughter is improving.

When my grandfather died, grandmother continued with her work for St Francis Church and from time to time I would go with her to morning service. She loved to walk through the park, keeping to the south side of the river Bourn, and in spring-time she would be delighted to see the first tiny snowdrops when they appeared on the grassy bank. She managed widowhood with a determination only someone with her strength of character and faith could muster.

The Old Farm Inn

Situated at the corner of Linden Road and Bournville Lane, The Old Farm Inn was originally Bournbrook Farm. The old farm buildings were re-modelled at the beginning of the century, the architect being W. Alexander Harvey, and it was henceforth known as 'Ye Olde Farm Inn'.

For many years during the latter part of the 19th century it was known locally as 'Froggatt's Farm' and was tenanted by Mrs Sarah Froggatt and her step-son William. Mrs Froggatt lived at the farm from 1864 until her death in 1899. Mr K. A. Newman writing in the Autumn 1991 edition of *The Carillon* (Bournville Village News) writes:

> Locally Mrs Froggatt had a great reputation as a herbalist and curer of ailments and injuries. In the early days of the chocolate factory there was no Works Surgery so factory workers injured in the course of their work were sent to the Farm to receive treatment from Mrs Froggatt. One person who sought Mrs Froggatt's help was 'Frederick the Frenchman' who was Head Confectioner at Cadbury's. Each summer he would spend a day at 'Woodbrooke' making jams and fruit syrups for the Cadbury household. Unfortunately Frederick suffered a bad scald to his arm which no doctor seemed able to heal. However

a visit to Mrs Froggatt and an application of her herbal preparations effected an immediate cure. Many of Mrs Froggatt's preparations were in great demand locally especially her famous salve for cuts and bruises which was known as 'Black Jack' ointment.

Bournbrook Farm kept a variety of farm animals including chickens and pigs. Once a week William Froggatt would go to the factory kitchen to collect two bucketsful of pig swill which he would carry home by a yoke over his shoulders. The Farm also kept a herd of dairy cows which grazed in a field behind the Farm. This field stretched from the corner of Linden Road and Bournville Lane to the brook in what is now Bournville Park. In 1883 William Froggatt rented the field to the Bournville Cricket Club who used it as a pitch until the present Men's Recreation Ground was opened in 1896.

The buildings to the rear of the Farm were referred to as 'The Lofts' and they were used by The Adult School, Boy Scouts, Camp-fire girls and similar organisations.

The Annual Report of the Bournville Village Council for the year 1904 carried an advertisement for 'Ye Old Farm Inn' which read:

> Hot Joints daily.
>
> Cyclists and Parties catered for.
>
> Mineral Waters and Refreshments.
>
> Horses taken in to bait.
>
> Cigars and Tobacco.
>
> PROPRIETOR. J. Bodycote.

No mention of intoxicating liquor, you notice.

A booklet entitled *The Bournville Village Trust* and dated 1901, is where I found the following:

> The Deed of Foundation of the Bournville Village Trust includes a clause relating to the sale of intoxicating liquor which provides that no house or building shall be used for such sale except under the following conditions. That the unanimous consent of all the Trustees in writing shall be a necessary precedent to the grant of the licence or other permit, and such consent shall be given, withheld, or have any condition as to

Linden Road with the Old Farm Inn just visible on the left.

The interior of the Old Farm Inn. Early 1900's.

The Old Farm Inn with nos. 106-102 Linden Road.

hours and quantities of sale, or any other matters attached thereto as the Trustees may determine. Further, all net profit arising from the sale of intoxicating liquor shall be devoted to securing for the village community recreation and counter attractions to the liquor trade as ordinarily conducted. The Trustees shall endeavour to act bearing in mind the Founder's 'intention that the sale, distribution, or consumption of intoxicating liquor shall be entirely suppressed if such suppression does not in the opinion of the Trustees lead to greater evils'.

To this day you will not find a Public House or Off-Licence in Bournville.

*Fircroft Junior
Adult School,
1913.*

*Reverse side of
photograph.*

THE FIRCROFT JUNIOR ADULT SCHOOL

would like you to add to their number,
and can ensure you a hearty welcome.
Will you turn up on Sunday next at
the Loft, Bournville Lane, at 9 a.m.

Camp-fire girls, July 4th 1914.

Ruskin Hall

The foundation stone for Ruskin Hall (situated at the corner of Linden Road and Woodbrooke Road) was laid by Lord Avebury on 21st October 1902 and the building was completed in 1903 at a cost of £3,263 13s. 4d., most of which was contributed by Mr and Mrs George Cadbury.

The Ruskin Society, the members of which acknowledged John Ruskin's sincere desire to promote the well-being of the people, was responsible for the project in the first instance but, although it collected funds it found itself unable to finance the scheme. As the building neared completion it was handed over to the Bournville Village Trustees and by agreement a Management Committee was appointed consisting of representatives of The Ruskin Society, Bournville Village Trust and the Bournville Village Council. For a time the premises were used as a school. The 1906 report of the Bournville Village Council has a paragraph which reads thus;

> Ruskin Hall has again proved of great value as a rallying point for social intercourse, and when it becomes possible to transfer

Ruskin Hall.

Ruskin Hall. A class of children with their teacher before the schools were built in 1906.

the temporary Infants' School to a new school building a great extension of its usefulness may be confidently anticipated.

The Infants' School was built in 1910 and from that year Ruskin Hall has been a centre for the study of Arts and Crafts.

In 1911, when Kings Norton Urban District Council (of which Bournville was a part) was absorbed by the City of Birmingham it was agreed the Education Committee of the City should take over the day to day running of Ruskin Hall. Since that time the administration and finances of the School have been in the hands of the City, though the control of the building is vested in its Management Committee.

The building was extended in 1927/28 at a cost of £5,000. Further need for enlargement of the premises was made known in 1939. Plans were prepared but war prevented building operations. A small potters' room was built in 1946. By 1957 yet another Extension Fund Appeal was sent out requesting £22,000, of which £7,500 had already been promised. The new rooms were built and were officially opened by Mr G. Trenchard Cox, CBE, MA (Director of the Victoria and Albert Museum), on 10th June 1958. The programme of events for that day tells us the extensions provide space for pottery, modelling and carving, general crafts, life-drawing, a staff common room, students' canteen and kitchen.

51

Friends' (Quaker) Meeting House

Bordering Bournville Village Green on its north side is the Friends' Meeting House, which when built in 1905 was designed to accommodate 400 people. At that time Hazel Road ran along the east side of the Green but it was closed in 1927 and made way for the Lime tree avenue which runs from the Meeting House across the Green to the main entrance of the Day Continuation College. The Green as we see it today was started in 1928 and completed in 1931.

The Meeting House is an attractive building; the main hall has a high wooden ceiling, and in recent years extensions have been tastefully added to the original construction. It has been used continuously each Sunday since the first Meetings were held there in September 1905. For many years it was the only place of public worship in Bournville and George and Elizabeth Cadbury were well aware of the needs of those who were not Quakers and for this reason provision was made for a passage from the Bible to be read early on in the Meeting before settling down into silent worship waiting before God. This arrangement continued until after the Second World War, when younger members of the Meeting asked that the Bible reading, which they felt had become a formal stereotyped practice, should be discontinued. Richenda Scott in her biography of Elizabeth M. Cadbury writes;

> The Meeting for Worship at Bournville was the centre of Elizabeth's religious life; every Sunday, morning and evening, she attended it faithfully when at home, taking a leading part in the vocal ministry. Her contributions were nearly always connected with some event of the week with which she had been concerned, some experience encountered in her dealings with people in the course of her many activities, but right to the end remained lucid, clear-cut, and incisive – never lapsing into the long and rambling discourse which is so often characteristic of the elderly speaker. Above all they were rooted in her clear and living faith in the goodness and the guidance of God.

Richenda Scott continues;

> The centre and core of the Quaker experience and expression of faith lies in the Meeting for Worship. To Elizabeth, the Friends' method of waiting together in silence before God offered the widest field for spiritual growth and opportunity for

Exterior.

THE FRIENDS' MEETING HOUSE, BOURNVILLE.

Interior (before the installation of an organ).

adventure. If it were rightly held, she said, the Meeting demanded of its members a great unselfishness. So many came desiring something for themselves, or with their minds burdened with problems which would face them in the coming week, and were not really prepared to wait for the guidance of the Holy Spirit and communion with the living God. She pleaded for a liberty which would allow expression in a hymn of praise and thanksgiving, for, without desiring any set programme of service, she felt that Friends lost much by omitting all music from their gatherings. In the Meeting at Bournville one hymn at least was sung during the hour of worship, and any member was free to ask for a hymn which he felt would give voice to the experience of the Meeting at that moment.

When Elizabeth Cadbury died in December 1951, two memorial services were held, the one at Bournville Meeting House being a gathering of relatives and intimate friends; this took the form of a Quaker Meeting for Worship. The other, a public gathering, was held in one of the large dining-rooms at Cadbury's Bournville Works. I turn again to Richenda Scott's biography for the following:

> More than 2,500 people came together to render her a last act of homage. All classes, all shades of political opinion, and nearly all branches of the Christian faith were represented in that congregation. Lord Justice Birkett gave the address, drawing on his long years of friendship with Elizabeth Cadbury to recall her personality and her ceaselessly active life. Linking the names of George and Elizabeth Cadbury, because 'they are inseparably joined together' he emphasised that:

> > For thirty years after that association ended, Dame Elizabeth carried on the private and public work they had together inaugurated, with the same practical idealism, the same vision, the same zeal, and the same complete devotion to the public and private good. Of both of them it must be said, however, that whilst they will be remembered for what they did, they will likewise be remembered for what they were. High purpose is the badge of the great man or woman ... George and Elizabeth Cadbury were great in purpose and great in achievement; but it was nevertheless a greatness of heart and mind that created the high purpose, and made all that marvellous outward achievement possible.

The Friends' Meeting House, 1950's.

A tree in the grounds of the Meeting House is decorated with coloured lights each Christmas. It is a Cedar of Lebanon and was planted by Dame Elizabeth Cadbury in 1948 to mark her 90th birth-day. Mr G. M. Davis of Harry Ward Ltd, wrote a short article in the Spring 1993 edition of *The Carillon*, Bournville Village News, 23, and I am indebted to him for allowing me to reprint his article in full.

> After weeks of preparation, checking lamps and leads, repairing and repainting the Star, it was time to decorate the Christmas Tree. But this tree is 50 feet tall and is located outside the Friends' Meeting House on Bournville Green.

> As usual, the morning is cold and damp and still dark on the day of the installation. Whilst we prepare the 60 feet lengths of cable and fit the coloured lamps into the weatherproof

lampholders, the Bournville Village Trust gardeners are high in the air at the top of the tree securing a scaffolding pole to the tree trunk. They have the use of a Hire Tower. After the pole is secured, the Star is raised high into the air and placed into the top of the pole. Once this is in place the 18 down leads complete with coloured lamps is raised, three at a time, into the air and secured to the bottom of the Star, and then draped down equally around the tree.

At the bottom of the tree is a large electric cupboard which has been linked to the electric supply within the Friends' Meeting House. It is complete with its own meter. The cables are then connected to the appropriate fused circuits.

By 3 o'clock we are ready for the final test. All the lights burst into life ready for the children leaving Bournville Junior and Infants School at 3.30 p.m.

How appropriate that a tree, planted by Dame Elizabeth Cadbury who, according to Richenda Scott, 'With children maintained a direct and frank relationship, neither sentimental nor condescending', should be decorated at Christmas, by so doing spreading joy to young and old alike.

The Schools

Situated at the corner of Linden Road and Woodbrooke Road the first school was built, in 1906, to accommodate 540 children and was a gift of Mr and Mrs George Cadbury, with a proposal to build another block for 270 infants at a later date.

There were six classrooms for 50 children each and six for 40 each. Four hundred and twenty children turned up to enrol on the first day, 23rd April 1906.

The Hall is remembered by all who have been pupils or staff of the school, for the 16 scenes from the New Testament that are depicted on its walls. In the booklet *Bournville Junior School - the First Eighty Years* we learn that two cartoon sketches drawn by Mary Sargant Florence in preparation for the frescoes are owned by the Tate Gallery. The works were painted directly on to specially prepared cement panels and are the work of Mrs Florence and Miss Creighton McDowell (daughter of the then Bishop of London), both well known fresco painters. With time the condition of the frescoes began to deteriorate but happily, in 1984, they were tastefully restored by the Perry Lithgo Partnership of

The Schools with the original School Tower.

*Taken from inside
the Entrance to the
Meeting House.*

Juniors.

Chipping Norton, Oxfordshire, after a generous grant was made by the George Cadbury Fund.

As proposed, the Infants' School was built in 1910, the foundation stone being laid by Ursula Cadbury, the youngest daughter of George and Elizabeth Cadbury. In 1938 a building to house two reception classes was erected on the remaining piece of land allocated for the schools. It can be seen by those who walk through the adjacent parkway. In 1906 my mother gave a talk to the Parent/Teachers Association on the occasion of the school's Diamond Jubilee. A print-out of that talk can be found in the appendices.

An unusual feature of the Bournville Junior School is the carillon of 48 bells on the roof of the School tower, one of the finest of the 14 carillons in the British Isles. A carillon is a musical instrument played from a 'baton' keyboard, known as a clavier. Unlike the bells in a traditional English change-ringing tower which swing through an arc of 360 degrees, the bells in a carillon are hung stationary and are sounded by clappers operated from the clavier, in a similar way to the tracker-action on an organ. Like an organ, the carillon also has a pedal keyboard. A wide range of music is playable on the carillon and the carilloneur can play with expression, like a pianist, varying the tempo and dynamics.

Infants.

The original home of the carillon is the Low Countries of Belgium, Holland and France, where the bells and towers have been prominent features of townscapes and municipal life for over 300 years. The Dutch have a saying:– 'Good schools and good bells are two signs of a well-managed city'. This may have been at the back of George Cadbury's mind when he decided to donate a carillon to the village of Bournville in 1906. Twenty-two bells were installed in the turret of the N.W. corner of the tower of the new village schools. His inspiration was the famous carillon which he heard during a visit to the town of Bruges in Belgium.

In 1923, 15 new bells were added, and a further five in 1925. These were given by the Cadbury family in memory of George Cadbury who died in 1922. A major reconstruction took place in 1934 when all except four bells were recast and six more bells added, including the very fine 64-cwt. bass bell on which the hours are sounded, and the smallest bell, weighing only 12 lbs. The north west turret, being no longer large enough to house all the bells, was removed and the bells hung in an open frame in the centre of the tower roof, protected only by a cupola supported on eight pillars. Only one of the original bells has survived, and it is inscribed as follows:–

The lawn – Bournville Infants' School – looking south.

Given by George Cadbury, 1906, to the village of Bournville. When'er the sweet Church bell peals over the hill and dell, may Jesus Christ be praised.

Recitals are given on Sundays in the summer, and it is also played for some local weddings, on School 'occasions', and on most Friday evenings in term.

The automatic clock chimes play on only eight bells. The tunes are known as 'The Guildford Chimes', and were composed by George Williams in 1843. From the earliest days of the school, it was the tradition that on their last day, children should stand underneath the bells as the clock struck 12 noon. The clock dials are the original ones, and incorporate the Latin motto, *carpe diem* (seize the present opportunity). Children also learned to sing the following words to the chime tunes:–

First Quarter: *Hear us, O Lord.*

Second Quarter: *Hear and answer these our prayers.*

Third Quarter: *We beseech Thee, hear and answer these our prayers, O Lord.*

60

View from the School Tower – looking south.

Fourth Quarter: *We beseech Thee, hear and answer these*
our prayers, O Lord.
And may Thy Holy Spirit dwell with us
for evermore.

Before the 1934 construction, there were also two chime barrels, operated automatically, which played the following tunes at three-hourly intervals:–

No.1 (Hymn Tunes)	*New every morning is the love*	*(Melcombe)*
	The day is past and over	*(St Anatolius)*
	Come sing with holy gladness	*(Ellacombe)*
	The day Thou gavest	*(St Clement)*
No. 2 (National Songs)	*The Country Garden*	
	(The Vicar of Bray)	*English*
	Will ye no come back again?	*Scottish*
	The Harp that once	*Irish*
	Jenny Jones	*Welsh*

The present day School Tower.

Bournville Carillon – *Inscriptions on the Bells*

The bells are listed in order of weight – lightest first. Nos. 4 to 41 were recast in 1934 by Gillett and Johnson. Nos. 42, 43, 45 and 47 were cast by John Taylor and Co. During 1987/88 the bells were silenced for emergency repair work to be carried out, thus ensuring the safety of the structure: Total cost £91,000.

Bells 1, 2 and 3 *Given in memory of George Cadbury by his wife, E.M.C. and son, G.C. 1934.*

Bells 2 to 21 No inscription.

Bell 22	*Musicam docet amor.*
23	*Adoramus te.*
24	*Benedicimus te.*
25	*Laudamus te.*
26	*Ora et vigila.*
27	*Per crucem ad stellas.*
28	*Adite et venite.*
29	*Non clamor sed amor cantat in aure dei.*
30	*Servite domine in laetitia.*
31	*Gloria in excelsis deo.*
32	*Goodwill toward men.*
33	*On earth peace.*
34	*Life means-learning to abhor the false and love the true.*
35	*Jesus be our speed.*
36	*Peace and good neighbourhood.*
37	*Ring out the false, ring in the true.*
38	*Ring out the old, ring in the new.*
39	*Praise to the Holiest in the height, and in the depths be praise.*
40	*Ring out the darkness of the land, ring in the Christ who is to be.*
41	*In memory of George Cadbury, who died 24th October 1922. His son George gave 15 bells to complete this carillon, 1923.*
42	*Given by George Cadbury, 1906, to the Village of Bournville. When'er the sweet church bell peals over hill and dale, may Jesus Christ be praised.*
43	*Ring in the common love of God. E.M.C. and G.C. June 1925.*
44	Same as 1, 2 and 3.
45	*Break forth into joy and sing together. E.M.C. and G.C. June 1925.*

46	Same as 1, 2 and 3.
47	*In memory of George Cadbury who loved the sound of bells. This bell is given by his wife, Elizabeth May, 1925.*
48	Same as 1, 2 and 3.

The Beeches

A large house, situated in Selly Oak Road at a point just below Bournville Lane, is 'The Beeches'. It was built to provide holiday accommodation for children from the slum areas of Birmingham. I refer to the author Richenda Scott's biography of Elizabeth Cadbury where it is written:

> The opportunity of providing holidays for children from the slum quarters of Birmingham was made possible by the building of a house, The Beeches, for this purpose in 1908.

An aerial view of The Beeches, 1950's.

Several years before, in 1895, George and Elizabeth Cadbury, with the vivid realisation of the crowded, dreary homes in which many of their adult-school members lived, decided that they would buy a house near Bournville to which the children at least could be invited to spend their holidays in happy and healthy surroundings. During the summer months, with the aid of members of the Women's Class at Severn Street, they were enabled to lodge and entertain relays of children, 30 at a time. 'Two splendid people were appointed to help with this fascinating plan' wrote Elizabeth of the scheme. The children called them 'Father and Mother Cole' and learned to love them devotedly.

On the evening of arrival each child was weighed and bathed, and if necessary given new clothes. (In the early years of this venture Mrs Cole sometimes found that children had been sewn in for the winter – that is, they never had their clothes removed.) Mr and Mrs Cole found also that most of the children had been used to being given 'a piece' when running in from school, and taking it into the streets to eat it. For the first day or two the children were not very hungry, but after settling down, appetites became huge and plate after plate of good things disappeared.

This, with the fresh air, and regular sleep brought about almost incredible improvement in health and in addition the weight. It was a great joy to welcome the children to tea at the Manor once a fortnight. Mr and Mrs Cole had a beautiful collie dog called Bob and an interesting grey parrot, and the children, almost without knowing it, absorbed lessons of kindness to animals.

So the children returned to their homes, not only well and vigorous, but with the experience of a real home life and of wholesome fun in beautiful surroundings.

During the winter months women from the Salvation Army were invited for a holiday to The Beeches and to enjoy a period of rest.

The new house, especially built for the purpose of a holiday home with its greater possibilities for usefulness, was a source of interest and concern to Elizabeth Cadbury. Her care for the amusement and the rebuilding of both body and mind of the children and adults who found sanctuary there was another constant claim upon her time and her imagination.

The Beeches was put to varied uses in the testing times that lay ahead. From 1914-1918 it became a war hospital, and for a time it housed the girls' classes of the Day Continuation Schools.

Between the wars it was used as a residential training centre for unemployed women from all parts of the country who were members of National Service Clubs.

During the Second World War it housed the staff and students of Hillcroft Working Women's College, evacuated from Surbiton in Surrey, and when they returned home it was used as a hostel for students attending Birmingham University.

Also at that time 'The Beeches Singers' (a madrigal group to which Laurence and Joyce Cadbury belonged) met there to sing together. It was thought important to sustain the arts, especially when the Luftwaffe made it dangerous to go down into the city centre at night. Subsequently it was taken over by Cadbury Brothers and was a college for members of the retail grocery and confectionery trades. At the present time it is run by the Kalamazoo group as a centre for management training.

The Woodlands

During the early 1900's the Crippled Children's Union of Birmingham would bring out to the fields of Manor Farm some of the little patients 150 at a time, so that they might lie in the grass and revel in the country sights and sounds for just a few hours.

In 1909 George Cadbury bought a large house situated on the other side of the Bristol Road from the Manor House and gave it to be used as a hospital for crippled children. It was opened on June 22nd of that year. To start with there was room for 37 beds – even the stables had been converted for use as a ward. First extensions were added in 1914.

With the amalgamation of the Birmingham Cripples' Union and the Royal Orthopaedic and Spinal Hospital for Adults in 1925 the hospital was henceforth known as the Royal Cripples' Hospital. Arrangements were made for patients from the orthopaedic hospital in Newhall Street, Birmingham, to be moved to The Woodlands.

The Woodlands, 1926. The room with the blinds is the Operating Theatre.

The Woodlands, Royal Orthopaedic Hospital (opened 22nd June 1909).
The original building can be seen in the foreground.

A further extension was built and was opened by the then Duchess of York, now Queen Elizabeth the Queen Mother, in November 1929. By that time there was accommodation for 100 patients.

Provision was made for long-stay children to be educated. The Hospital school was, and still is, recognised by the Board of Education.

I have always understood there was a Scout Troop within the hospital but unfortunately have been unable to confim this. However a close friend of mine, who is himself a past patient of the Woodlands, recalls Scouts visiting patients and teaching them how to tie different types of knots, and to recognise animal paw prints and suchlike. Could it be the group involved were not registered by the Scouting Movement, but that the visiting Scouts were from local Northfield, Bournville or Kings Norton troops and were doing their bit to brighten the lives of young long-stay patients.

During the 1914-1918 war, at the time France was falling to the German Reich, many patients were evacuated from a hospital in Ostend, Belgium, and 40, together with their Matron and three nurses, found themselves at The Woodlands. Richenda Scott, in her biography of Elizabeth Cadbury writes:

> They quickly settled down into the routine of the English hospital, forming friendships, despite the barriers of language, with English patients and staff; their own matron remained throughout the five years of the war, working harmoniously with Miss Fanny Smith, her English counterpart. It says much for the skill and tact of both women that no word of disagreement, no hint of friction, arose throughout that period. The majority of the patients were nursed back to health, and found work in the locality; some married and settled down in Birmingham. Only one was left as a patient when war was ended and the matron could return home.

On 23rd November 1940 at 1a.m. the hospital was struck by a bomb and two very valued Nursing Sisters were killed. A telephone call from the Matron at 7.30a.m. that day told Elizabeth Cadbury of the tragedy which had befallen the hospital, and she was over there shortly afterwards, despite her 82 years, 'to uphold Matron and her Staff, and go round the wards again, to show our concern for the patients'. Elizabeth Cadbury's diary records:

The raid started at 7 p.m. on 22nd November and continued for most of the night. The Manor suffered broken windows and lack of gas and water.

As a result of the bombing, 38 children were sent to the Forelands Hospital at Bromsgrove, Worcestershire, and 60 adults returned to their homes, but 140 remained in the damaged building, and the usual round of hospital life continued.

Elizabeth Cadbury was Chairman of House Committee from its inception until the hospital was taken over by the State in 1948. Throughout her life she visited The Woodlands almost daily. She would sometimes take her two small dogs whose gambols and tricks were a source of amusement for the young patients.

At the present time The Woodlands has 149 beds and the wonderful work of its surgeons, doctors, and nurses is recognised world-wide, and many people have to be very grateful for treatment received there. How sad then to find, that, along with many other such fine institutions that were born out of the concern of a forward looking pioneer, it should find itself in the firing-line of proposed closure.

The Rest House

The Rest House is situated in the centre of Bournville Village Green. Modelled on Dunster Yarn Market, Somerset, it was erected in 1913 by the employees of Cadbury Brothers Ltd at Bournville and in all parts of the world, to commemorate the silver wedding of George Cadbury and his wife Elizabeth. Opened in 1914 a mural tablet in the Rest House Reeds:

> This Rest House was erected to commemorate the silver wedding of
>
> ### MR AND MRS GEORGE CADBURY
>
> by the employees of Cadbury Bros Ltd at Bournville and in all parts of the world as a lasting memorial of esteem and affection, as an expression of gratitude for the unceasing interest in their welfare and in admiration of manifold social services to the world at large.
>
> ### 1888-1913

The interior carved stone panels record events in the development of the Cadbury Works and the Village. Two record the founding of the Bridge Street Works in 1831 by John Cadbury, and the founding of

The Rest House, late 20's.

Memorial Service for George Cadbury, 1922.

the Bournville Works by Richard and George Cadbury in 1879. The interior is richly decorated in reds, green and gold.

George Cadbury died on 24th October 1922, and was cremated at Perry Barr on Saturday October 28th. His ashes were gathered in an urn which was later placed in the Columbarium at The Friends' Meeting House.

I turn to Mr A. G. Gardiner's *Life of George Cadbury* for an account of the memorial service held at Bournville.

It was on the Village Green at Bournville that the most significant tribute to George Cadbury's life was paid. Around the Rest House in the centre of The Green there gathered some 16,000 people to pay homage to a great memory. The Rest House was enveloped in masses of flowers from hundreds of

71

The Village Green, 1990.

friends, public institutions, religious bodies, among them two which would have given George Cadbury peculiar pleasure, those from the Austrian children he had befriended at Bournville, and from the children of the Tyrol. The former bore the inscription, 'To the revered memory of Mr George Cadbury, the life-long friend of all nations. "Blessed are the peacemakers."' It was a day of radiant beauty, and while the great throng of mourners was assembling, the favourite hymn tunes of George Cadbury were played on the Carillon that had been one of his many gifts to the Village, and at intervals sacred music was rendered by the Works Choir and Band. The service was simple and moving, and it was indicative of the appeal of George Cadbury's life that it touched its deepest note in the hymn for the children 'I think when I read that sweet story of old'. The tribute to George Cadbury's memory was delivered by Dr Henry T. Hodgkin, who had recently returned from China, and who was assisted in the conduct of the service by Mr John William Hoyland and the Vicar of Bournville, the Reverend A. Creed Meredith.

To commemorate the 150th anniversary of the birth of George Cadbury, the Birmingham Civic Society put up a special commemorative plaque on the Rest House in October 1989, in the presence of the Lord Mayor of the City, Councillor Frederick Chapman, the Lady Mayoress, and the Founder's granddaughter, Mrs Veronica Wootten, as well as members of the Civic Society. The plaque bears the inscription 'The Bournville Building Estate created in 1895 by George Cadbury'.

Selly Manor

Selly Manor is a house of the 14th century. Records found in connection with the house concern a family by the name of Jowette who were Lords of the Manor between 1327 and 1400. It is said that Richmond slept at the house on his way to Bosworth Field prior to the battle; also Cromwell, and Catesby, of Gunpowder Plot fame.

Selly Manor, pre-1929.

Originally the house stood in Bournbrook Road, about a mile to the north east of Bournville. It was removed and rebuilt between 1913/1916 under the supervision of W. Alexander Harvey, Bournville Village Trust Architect. Gradually over the years items of furniture and artefacts relating to the date of its origin were purchased by Laurence Cadbury, George Cadbury's son, and now it is one of the main buildings to be visited throughout the year by folk from near and far. The present Curator, Elizabeth M. Henslowe, when writing to local residents in January 1991 stated:

> Since Selly Manor opened to the public in 1917 the cost has been borne by the Bournville Village Trust. In the early days, after the house had been newly re-built, the need for maintenance was minimal, in recent years, however, the cost of up-keep has become a more significant matter. Therefore, the Board of Management of Selly Manor have decided that the time has come for the Museum to become financially independent gradually over the next few years. In order to achieve this independence the decision has been made to begin charging for admission, so that from the day we re-open, the charge for adults will be £1.00 and children 50p. Parties of school children and their attendant adults and other students on organised educational visits will be free.

In Issue 16 of *News from the Trust*, December 1994, The Curator of Selly Manor reported that she was confident 1994 would turn out to have been a very good year for the Museum. It had had 14,000 visitors, many of them school children having a guided tour of the half-timbered houses for the 'Tudors and Stuarts' part of their National Curriculum course. The same report tells us that from 1995, with the exception of the schools on the Bournville Estate whose pupils would continue to get free entry, all other schools visiting the Museum would be charged 50p per child with teachers and adult attendants free. It is hoped this arrangement will help to shift the burden of cost of running the Museum away from the Trust. Time will tell.

Minworth Greaves

Minworth Greaves House stood, for centuries, by the side of the Kingsbury Road between Curdworth and Minworth (Warwickshire), and must have been a house of some importance with several acres of land adjacent, possibly including a portion of the historic 'Curdworth

Fields', where the first skirmish of the Civil War between King Charles and the Parliament occurred on September 12th 1642.

The building was acquired in 1911 and the re-siting commenced in 1929 and was completed in 1932. The re-building and restoration was carried out by Mr Charles H. Mitchell, Contractor, of Tamworth, under the direction of W. Alexander Harvey. It is an example of the cruck method of building and shows that angularly bent trees were used in the Midlands. Visitors will notice the principals are in one piece from the ground to the roof, unlike the 'post and truss' method used in Selly Manor. Trunks of Oak were split, and pairs mounted on a stone base and brought together at their apex by a ridge tree. Tie braces and wind-braces were fastened together by wooden pegs to give extra strength to the framework.

In addition to raising as much money as possible to offset the cost of running the above buildings, the Museum Committee also allow charitable organisations to stage fund-raising events in Minworth Greaves from time to time. During 1994 a three-day Flower Festival was held, resulting in £1,200 being raised for Midlands Aid for Rwanda.

Situated at the corner of Sycamore and Maple Roads, on the eastern side of the Village Green, the Museum is well worth a visit.

Bournville Parish Church

The foundation stone for Bournville Parish Church, St Francis of Assisi, was laid by Lord Robert Cecil in July 1924. The building, built by public subscription, cost £16,500 including furnishings. The consecration ceremony took place on 21st November 1925. The Bournville Council Year Book for 1927 carries the following account of that day:

> Residents in the Village, and many outside, have shown a wide interest in the building of Bournville's new church. (Up until this date the present church hall had been used for religious services.) The church, having almost reached completion – in as far as it is at present intended to build – was consecrated on Saturday 21st November, the ceremony being performed by the Bishop of Birmingham, Dr E. W. Barnes. There were also present Canon Blofeld, who acted as the Bishop's Chaplain, and the Archdeacons of Birmingham and Aston, together with other

well-known Midland clergy, the architects, Mr W. Alexander Harvey and Mr W. Graham Wicks, and many connected with the church or who have been associated with the scheme.

Following the entry of the Bishop into the church, after he had first, in the customary manner, knocked three times at the door, the petition for consecration was presented by the Reverend W. Davison. The 122nd Psalm and the hymn, 'Come, Holy Ghost, our souls inspire' were then sung, followed by the Lord's Prayer and the hymn 'We love the place, O God.' During the singing of the last named, the Bishop, wardens, and the official clergy proceeded to the font, the pulpit, the lectern, and the chancel, where an appropriate passage of Scripture was read by the Archdeacon, the Bishop pronouncing the sentence of consecration. After this impressive ceremony the clergy returned to their seats and the Bishop to the altar, which they dedicated. Taking the crozier in his hand he next pronounced the consecration of the church under the name of St Francis of Assisi.

Having signed the deed, the Bishop returned it with the petition to the Registrar to be enrolled and preserved on the registry of the diocese.

Dr Barnes, who took his text: 'I was glad when they said unto me: Let us go into the House of the Lord' (Psalm xxii.v.1), said that they were passing through a period of spiritual turmoil. Faith in Christ had become weaker, but he believed the tide would eventually turn, for man needed religious truth in all walks of life. 'We can rejoice,' he said, 'that even now progress is being made, and that this church is a sign of spiritual vitality. Fourteen years ago,' he observed, 'a handful of people gathered in house for a week-night service, but now there is a congregation of over 500.'

Drawing attention to the urgent need for increasing the number of churches in Birmingham to meet the needs in the rapidly growing suburbs, Dr Barnes said that there were, in the diocese, one-and-a-half million people and 159 parishes, or about 10,000 people to each parish. If half a million pounds were available to erect and endow 30 additional churches he did not think the existing need would be adequately met.

Dr Barnes referred to the friendly interest and sympathy shown in the work by members of other denominations, and in

Bournville Parish Church, St Francis of Assisi.

particular, by the Society of Friends. The knowledge that they had received such splendid help was one of the happy associations of that festival. Members of the house of Cadbury had individually and collectively given as much as £3,000 to the cause. Of the £13,500 required, only a comparatively small sum was outstanding.

After the ceremony many of the clergy and others attending were entertained to tea at Westholme by Mr and Mrs Edward Cadbury.

By 1927, an organ, previously housed in the Dining Room at their works, was kindly given by Messrs Cadbury Brothers and was consecrated by the Archdeacon of Birmingham on January 2nd. The instrument was three-manual and had well over 30 stops. Mr J. N. Southall was appointed Organist and Choirmaster. The congregation numbers were well maintained and extra chairs were frequently needed for Evening Service, proof positive that the Church had met a real need in the neighbourhood. The furnishing of the Chancel was under way and an order had been placed for Choir Stalls. A sum of £644 was raised at the annual Bazaar.

Records show that in 1928/29 the Church Sunday School had at least 350 children and young people on the books. Plans were in process for the erection of a permanent pulpit and altar, and the Bazaar made a net profit of £670, resulting in the paying off of the last £800 of the loan of £2,000 two years before it was necessary according to the terms of the loan.

The Reverend W. Davison wrote the following in the Bournville Council Year Book for 1930.

> In our Church life at Bournville we stand for no narrow, sectarian and partisan interests, but for full faith and worship of the Christian Church in all its manifold varieties. We have our own method and point of view, but we do not say that it is the only right way and that all others are wrong.
>
> Accordingly we not only extend the spirit of toleration to the varied groups in our own Church, but we welcome to our pulpit from time to time leading members of the Free Churches.
>
> Our relations with the Meeting House remain of the most cordial and friendly nature. During the year all three Clergy have accepted invitations to preach either at the Evening Meeting or the Brotherhood Service. We also acknowledge with due gratitude the sympathetic interest shown in our Church life by Mrs George Cadbury and other leaders of the Meeting House.

The previous year had seen a continuation of the furnishing of the Church and the order for the permanent pulpit and screen in stone with marble facings had been given. A Holy Communion Table had been given by the Parish Church of Birmingham. The Sanctuary furnishings, when completed, were dedicated by the Bishop of Birmingham and the occasion was used to plant eight silver birch trees in memory of eight men who had died during the building of the Church.

With the completion of the interior of the Church it was hoped an effective scheme to build permanent Porches and Vestries would be forthcoming. The cost was envisaged as being around £3,000.

No fewer than 59 candidates from the Bournville Parish were confirmed by the Bishop, Dr Barnes, in the presence of a crowded congregation on March 22nd, 1931.

It was in 1932 that the Porches were completed with the one facing north being surmounted by a carved figure representing St Francis. At the same time an effort was made to clear up and beautify the grounds of the Church. The iron railings were dismantled and replaced by a low wall which brought the Church into harmony with the Village Green.

In 1933 the Vicar, the Reverend W. Davison, was appointed to a living in Luton, Bedfordshire, and so Bournville welcomed the Reverend G. E. N. Molesworth. Bournville Council Year Book 1935 states:

> Mr Molesworth has felt that after the strenuous and excellent work of building with bricks and mortar of the last 10 years, probably the time has now arrived in which the Church life, together with the spiritual and devotional atmosphere, should be consolidated and our resources strengthened. In such an atmosphere of material efficiency and social well-being as the parish affords the Anglican Church has a very high standard to which she should strive to attain. Our work on the spiritual side must also count in the great movement of life.

The building of the Cloisters and Vestries was completed in 1937, just before the Coronation, and during Coronation week the Village Centre buildings were floodlit and were admired by visitors, many of whom had travelled long distances.

In 1938, when clouds of war were gathering, the Rev. Gilbert Molesworth gave the following message.

> Toleration, comprehensiveness and many different viewpoints, art, culture, and the relevance of Christianity in a perplexing world – all this is what we should like to offer, together with the simple homeliness which meets the intimacies of our domestic joys and sorrows. All this is helping to build our village history, and if it be acceptable and useful to the character of our community, we pray that the welfare of St Francis may be increasingly the concern and responsibility of the life of the Village.

Under the heading 'Items of interest for visitors to Bournville' the Parish Church of St Francis listed the following in 1940:

Services in the Parish Church of St Francis.

Sundays:	Holy Communion:	Every Sunday at 8 a.m.
	Sung Family Communion:	First Sunday at 10 a.m.
	Fourth Sunday	Sung Eucharist 11 a.m.
	Junior Church for Children	10 a.m.
	Matins and Sermon	11 a.m.
	Evensong and Sermon	6.30 p.m.
	Young People's Meeting	6.15 p.m.
	Sunday School, in Church Hall, for infants.	3 p.m.

Weekdays:	Holy Communion, third Wednesday	9.30 a.m.
	every Wednesday	7 a.m.
	or Saints' days	7 a.m.

Ten years later the advertisement read:

Services:

Holy Communion: every Sunday at 8 a.m. Last Sunday at 12 noon.
Sung Family Communion: first Sunday at 10 a.m.
 third Sunday Sung Eucharist, 11 a.m.
Junior Church for Children 10 a.m.
Matins and Sermon 11 a.m. (except 3rd Sunday),
Evensong and Sermon 6.30 p.m.
Sunday School. 10 a.m. in Church Hall, for Infants.

In addition the following organisations met at the Church Hall.

Mothers' Union	every second Monday in the month.
Young Wives' Fellowship	every Wednesday at 3 p.m.
Young People's Association (senior section)	every Tuesday evening.
Young People's Association (junior section), and St John's Ambulance Brigade,	every Wednesday evening.
Friday Forum	every Friday evening in the Winter

The *Bournville Estate Residents' Hand book* for 1970 tells us that the Chapel added in 1966 is in memory of the children of Laurence and Joyce Cadbury.

Services at that time were as follows:

Sundays	Holy Communion	8.15 a.m. and 9.30 a.m.
	Family Worship	10.30 a.m. Holy Communion first Sunday.
	Evensong	6.30 p.m.
	Sunday School	10.30 a.m. in the Church Hall.
Weekdays	Holy Communion	7 a.m. (Wednesday)
		9.30 a.m. (Thursday)
Saints' Days		7 a.m. (by announcement)

As the Estate grew other premises were used for Sunday worship, i.e. The Woodlands Park Hall. In the 30's Hay Green Methodist Church was built in Cob Lane, near the corner of Hay Green Lane, and with the more recent development of Shenley Green, the Anglican Church of St David's was erected.

Bournville has a thriving Council of Churches made up of representatives from varying denominations who seek to encourage Christian Unity by initiating joint activity and worship wherever possible.

The Day Continuation School

The Day Continuation School began its life on 6th October 1913 as a Day Class for Young employees, held in Stirchley Institute (Pershore Road at the junction of Bournville Lane) outside the Bournville boundaries. It was started by Cadbury Brothers Ltd who were joined by Morland and Impey Ltd of Northfield (now Kalamazoo Business Systems plc.). The junior employees of these firms were required as a condition of employment to attend for one half-day each week. By the end of the first year 209 boys and 476 girls had been enrolled. The school leaving age at the time was 14.

In 1914 the boys were removed to the Friends' Hall, Cotteridge. The girls remained at Stirchley until 1919, when they were transferred to The Beeches in Selly Oak Road, Bournville. The two schools were first referred to in 1917 as the Bournville Day Continuation School, from which time most graduate students attended for one whole day each week.

Built in 1925 on the northern side of the Village Green, the Day Continuation School was specially designed and calculated to create an 'academic atmosphere' by Bournville Village Trust architect J. R. Armstrong. The School was built by Cadbury Brothers Ltd, who leased the building to the City Education Authority. By so doing they retained the right to use the building for their own educational purposes out of ordinary school hours.

Students in 1925 totalled 1,850. During the time of the depression the numbers fell to just over 700 in 1930. However, as trade revived the number of students began to increase and by 1935 five firms and two municipal departments were making use of the facilities offered.

In 1949 Birmingham Education Authority changed the name from School to College. By 1953 there were some 1,800 students being sent by 60 employers, mostly for one whole day per week.

In 1959, the Old Boys' Association, which consisted largely of those men who were students in the 1920's, decided to disband, as their members were now scattered too far afield to have regular meetings. To mark their appreciation of what the College had done for them they presented a clock for the Entrance Tower.

In the period 1962-66 the College buildings on Bournville Green became too small to accommodate the fast-growing number of students and as a result various church halls, Institutes and wooden huts in the area were brought into use. Over 17 separate annexes within a mile radius were being used. It was to be 15 years before the College would be based on one site again.

The Day Continuation School – Bournville.

In 1973 the closure of some of the annexes began and in 1978 the buildings on Bournville Village Green were passed over to Bournville School of Arts and Crafts, and at the same time Bournville College took over the present Bristol Road site.

Now referred to as Bournville College of Further Education, with the logo 'Excellence in Action' it should be remembered that the College has had to face many problems during its lifetime and, one presumes, those who hold positions of responsibility for its future will doubtless meet similar hurdles. Mr David J. Ward, Principal of the College from 1978-1985, when writing in a book entitled *Bournville College of Education, 75 years of Continuity and Change 1913-1988*, suggested '*Recular pour mieux sauter* (Step-back, the better to lead forward) might well serve to mark the 25 years since the Golden Jubilee'. I believe the same could be said today.

Rowheath

The Bournville Council Year Book for 1925 carries the following article:

> Some 10 years ago land amounting to about 70 acres was purchased to provide additional playing grounds for Bournville employees.

> Owing to the war, the development of the grounds was postponed, but with the formation of the Works Departmental Games Association, the greatly increased demand for facilities led to the rapid development of the grounds. As time went on, further fields were converted into playing areas and as the whole of the grounds became more and more developed, plans were prepared for the laying out of a Garden Club, a scheme which would absorb nine acres out of the total 70 acres of land. The leading features of the Garden Club are the Central Pavilion, a large lawn and a model lake. Spaces have been reserved for the playing of clock-golf, croquet, etc. There are two open-air stages, one on either side of the extreme end of the lawn. The lawn has been largely used for dancing, while the provision of the model lake has resulted in the formation of a Model Yacht Club. The Central Pavilion is a prominent landmark, being situated on high ground. French windows open out from the front of the Pavilion on to a terrace which overlooks the lawn below.

Rowheath Housing, 1995.

Rowheath, 1928. Heath Road – the Pavilion can just be seen on the left in the distance.

Housing at Rowheath Solar Village, 1995.

Rowheath Pavilion, 1928.

A balcony extends on both sides of the building, giving on one side a view of the lake, through an avenue of trees planted on the lawn, and on the other, an extensive view of the countryside.

Inside the Pavilion accommodation is provided for about 450 players in 40 dressing rooms, the equipment including shower baths, wash-basins, etc.

There are also exterior and interior buffets, the former being provided for the convenience of players and spectators desiring light refreshment.

The playing grounds provide 14 Association pitches, 2 Rugby pitches, 5 hockey pitches, 16 cricket pitches, 31 tennis courts, 2 bowling greens and 2 croquet lawns. These are reserved for the use of employees and their wives and families. Employees may, however, take a friend by application for a special pass.

The same Year Book reports that:

Messrs Cadbury Brothers Ltd have made a new road across Rowheath Recreation Ground, which at the south-western end passes over an area of Trust land, giving frontage for about 30 houses. This road has been joined up with Hawthorne and Northfield Roads, thus connecting the Village of the Bournville Tenants Limited with Bournville.

A small Pavilion for women was built in the grounds in 1927.

During the winter season of 1926-27: *387 Association Football*
67 Rugby
and 142 Hockey matches were played.
In the summer season of 1927: *182 Cricket matches were played*
and app. 5,743 hours of tennis were played.
From September 1926 to August 1927 *approximately 17,000 players and officials took part in matches on Saturday afternoons.*

Elementary schools were allowed to use the grounds during work hours.

Approximately 16,470 persons attended the open-air concerts during the summer months.

During the Second World War a number of the football pitches were ploughed up and cultivated, providing cereal crops and vegetables.

In 1942, dancing on the lawn was organised as part of the 'Brighter Birmingham' campaign to encourage people to take their annual holidays at home, thus saving fuel for needed transport.

I recall one incident that happened on 'Rowheath Rec.', as it was affectionately called, on a Bank Holiday Monday in the 50's. I think it was at Easter-time. The weather that morning had been quite warm and humid, and by early afternoon it turned into a thunderstorm. We were suddenly alerted to the sound of a light aeroplane, circling round at quite a low altitude, and then silence. Before long news reached us that the pilot was a local man and had been flying back from Cardiff when bad weather closed in and the only building he could see that he recognised was Birmingham University Clock Tower. He decided the best thing to do was to try to land on Rowheath. This he did, successfully. The story goes that he contacted Castle Bromwich Aerodrome requesting permission to 'take-off' when the weather cleared, but his request was refused due to the close proximity of housing. Arrangements were made for a low-loader vehicle and mechanics to be sent to Rowheath, and when they arrived they removed the plane's wings and the aircraft finished its journey, unceremoniously, by road to Castle Bromwich. The incident was reported in all the papers next day and the pilot was the talk of the Village.

A similar happening had taken place on the Cadbury Brothers Mens' Recreation Grounds some 40 years earlier, but on that occasion the pilot had been expected.

In recent years 65 acres of land at Rowheath have been developed resulting in the provision of both privately owned dwellings and several housing schemes for the elderly and needy. I refer to these in greater detail in the section entitled 'Housing for the Needy'.

To give some idea of the many and varied sporting and community activities that have taken place at the Pavilion and the recreation grounds in recent years I quote the following from the Spring 1993 *Carillon*, Bournville Village News No. 23.

> There are approximately 25 community groups that use the Pavilion and the grounds regularly – and there is room for more. These include such diverse activities as Rugby, Soccer, Hockey, Cricket, Running, Bowling and Croquet to indoor activities such as Mother and Toddler groups, Playgroups, Tumble-Tots, Aerobics, Ballroom dancing, Tea dancing, Tap-dancing, Trinity Church.

In addition, the Pavilion is increasingly in demand as a centre for its bar and catering facilities.

From time to time there are a variety of social events which are open to the public such as fashion-shows, art exhibitions, circus, jazz and folk evenings, craft fairs, and band concerts.

I for one hope no further building development will take place in the Rowheath area, but that the Pavilion, parkland and sports grounds will remain a part of the one-tenth of the Estate laid out as open space as was originally intended by the Founder.

Bournville Model Yacht and Power Boat Club

The Club, founded in the mid 20's was a 'Works Society' of Cadbury Brothers with membership restricted to employees and relatives with a small percentage of Associate Members from elsewhere. The sailing water was the pond on Rowheath but the Club moved to the Valley Parkway in 1932 on completion of the specially constructed lake and boathouse.

Early in the 1950's the Club became independent of the Company and membership steadily increased. Usually there are about 100 active members and the Club has always been considered one of the premier clubs in the country. Over the years there have always been members who are among the top ranking enthusiasts in their skills of sailing, construction and designing. Both in sailing and power boats, members have won countless National Championships and leading designers have learnt their craft at the Valley Pool, and have been able to make significant contribution to full scale developments.

This tradition for excellence continues today, and with the advent of sophisticated radio control equipment the sport is enjoying an upsurge in popularity. Members of the Club travel extensively both at home and abroad representing their club and country.

The Yachting Pool, Valley Parkway

(Situated at the corner of Bournville Lane and Woodbrooke Road)

The Bournville Village Council Year Book dated 1934 carries an account of the opening of the Model Yachting Lake, and as this venue

The Pool, Rowheath Recreation Ground.

is frequented by many visitors to Bournville, I feel it necessary I should include the original report in its entirety.

THE NEW MODEL YACHTING LAKE

The opening of the new Model Yachting Lake was a notable occasion in Bournville history. To begin with, there was the widespread interest taken in its construction as an unemployment relief scheme, and secondly, it is a charming addition to the amenity of the Estate and district which will be used by and give pleasure to very many now and in the future. The scene on Saturday, August the 19th, was worthy of the occasion.

There were some 3,000 people gathered round the margin of the Lake when Mr and Mrs Edward Cadbury took their seats on the dais, accompanied by Mr C. W. Gillett, officers of the Bournville Model Yacht Club, officials of the Bournville Village Trust, together with Councillor MacDonald (Chairman of the Birmingham Parks Committee), and others interested in the scheme. Included in the company in the 'reserved' area were the

BOURNVILLE MODEL YACHT POOL

The men who have constructed the pool are arranging a programme for Saturday afternoon, 19th August, at the Allotments' Barn, Rowheath, with the co-operation of the Bournville Works Allotments Association and the instructors of the educational classes which the men have been attending throughout the period.

The programme will include tea for the men and their wives and families, open air sports and entertainments for the children and an exhibition of garden produce and handicrafts.

It is desired to meet the cost by gifts in money and in kind and your support is invited. If you can help, will you kindly complete and return the attached slip so that a representative may call upon you at your convenience.

To:

BOURNVILLE MODEL YACHT POOL
GATHERING FOR MEN ENGAGED ON CONSTRUCTION

I shall be pleased to give

and should be glad if a representative could call upon

me on   at the following address.

Signed _____

Address ___ _____

Please return this slip to the Education Dept., Bournville

or W.H. Meredith, No.2 Lodge, Bournville.

(Gifts of money may also be forwarded to these addresses)

90

unemployed men by whose efforts the Lake has been created, together with their wives and families.

Congratulatory messages were received from the Eastbourne and district Model Yacht Club, and from the Gosport Club, while the Fleetwood and Kettering Clubs were represented in the Regatta events, and officials of the Birmingham and Fleetwood Clubs were among the officers.

In introducing Mr Edward Cadbury, the Chairman, Mr W. H. Davey (Commodore of the Club), said how much they regretted that Mr P. S. Cadbury had been unable to preside that afternoon. It had been largely due to his enthusiasm that the Club had been started, when in 1922 a sailing pool had been constructed at the Rowheath Garden Club. Mr P. S. Cadbury, with Mr C. A. Harrison, as President and Secretary respectively of the Bournville Youths' Club, had been interested in providing some activity for boys to whom strenuous games did not particularly appeal, and from its small beginnings as a

Winter – Skating.
The Valley Park Yachting Pool, before the development of Woodbrooke Meadow.

THE VALLEY PARKWAY – YACHTING POOL, 1992.

Looking West.

Looking East.

sectional activity of the Youths' Club the Bournville Model Yacht Club had now grown to be one of the largest in the Kingdom, and was represented at most of the championship contests at Gosport and Fleetwood. The Rowheath Pool, while delightfully situated, had proved inadequate for the growing number of members, and so today they found themselves happy in the possession of the new Lake.

Mr Edward Cadbury briefly reviewed the history of the construction of the Lake by the Bournville Village Trust, with the co-operation of the Firm, as a scheme for the relief of unemployment in Birmingham. The work had been undertaken because it was neither essential, nor competitive, nor profit-making. It had provided employment for 64 men, representing 269 persons in all, who because of the length of time they had been out of work, or for other reasons, were ineligible for State Unemployment Benefit. They had been engaged on the work for $4\frac{1}{2}$ days per week, spending the remaining day at instructional classes. Although only 17 men had had any previous experience of work of the kind – excavating and moving soil and mud – none had given it up on that account. Mr Edward Cadbury also pointed out that further work was in progress nearby, in the construction of a road which would give further employment to some men for at least another two or three months. He thought the Scheme had been a great success and he hoped that similar schemes would be undertaken by employers elsewhere.

Turning to the men who had been engaged upon it, Mr Edward Cadbury said:

> I wish to thank you, on behalf of us all, for the way in which you have put your best into the job. Many, I know, were not accustomed to work of this kind, and found it very difficult to cope with it. I hope in the future you will feel that it is work of which you may be proud, and that it will bring you pleasant memories.

It must be remembered, the speaker went on, that what the unemployed wanted was not recreation but the opportunity to work for the community, so that they might feel they were a necessary part of it, and that they were giving the community valuable service.

In conclusion, Mr Edward Cadbury thanked Mr W. J. Miller, who has acted as foreman of the work, for the energy and patience with which he had carried it out.

Councillor G. F. MacDonald, speaking as President of the Birmingham Model Yacht Club and as Chairman of the Birmingham Parks Committee, after saying how indebted they all were to the Bournville Village Trust for providing that splendid amenity, said that the sport of model yacht racing was becoming increasingly popular. Unfortunately facilities were rather lacking in Birmingham, but he had done his best to press the claims of the sport. They had been hampered by financial considerations, but now it was going ahead by leaps and bounds. Quoting Portia, Councillor MacDonald said he was sure the Scheme had blessed those who gave it, it had certainly blessed those engaged in making it, and it would also bless those who would use it in years to come.

Mr Edward Cadbury then hoisted the house flag of the Firm and the Model Yacht Club's flag and declared the Lake open.

The Model Yachting Lake, to give it its formal title, is some 500 ft. x 150 ft. and was constructed on a very marshy piece of land, and as has already been mentioned the work involved was very hard, very few mechanical labour-saving devices being available at the time. The land was scheduled under the Town Planning Act as an open space; it was therefore envisaged that it would become a general amenity of the locality.

A Bournville Works publication entitled, *An Unemployment Relief Scheme. Notes on an Experiment made by the Bournville Village Trust 1932/33*, refers to the remuneration of the workers involved:

> Only those men were engaged who through length of the period of unemployment, or for other reasons, were not eligible for State Unemployment Benefit. The net wages paid were £1. 18s. 11d. per week plus a mid-day meal on four days a week. This sum is higher than would have been picked up under the State Unemployment Scheme, but lower than the wages of whole-time workers on regular development work. The wages must be considered in relation to the conditions under which the work was carried out and to the fact that it was neither essential, competitive, nor profit-making.

It would appear the engagement of workers proved difficult due to the widely differing circumstances. There were those who had been continually unemployed and others who were frequently out of work. There were married men, and single men with domestic responsibilities, or in distress without homes; men with children who had small earnings inadequate to their own support; those in receipt of low transitional payments owing to supplementary income and those with 'nil' determinations which might indicate high family earnings, and there were those likely to benefit from attendance at classes.

As the foregoing report has said, 64 men were engaged. They worked in rotation with 51 at work and 13 attending classes. The men came from nine different districts of Birmingham; 29 labourers, 17 navvies, 16 tradesmen and 2 were salesmen. The average length of time employed was 15 months.

The Bournville Works publication goes on to say:

> Family circumstances differed greatly. Those taken into account included average income per head after paying rent, thus balancing small against large families. The lowest for small families was 1s. 3d. per head (a man, wife, and three children under 14 years); the lowest among the large families was 1s. 6½d. per head (man, wife, and six children under 14 years). The relation of rent to food, etc., expenditure was also examined, as a number of men were found to be spending a very high percentage of their income on rent or house purchase owing to previous commitments, and to the fact that they were unable to move, as landlords would not accept unemployed men as new tenants. The small rentals ranged from 4s. 3d. to 6s. 3d. per week, giving an expenditure per head on food, etc., of 4s. 2d. to 4s. 7d. per week, though in one family (man, wife, and one child) the rent was 5s. 4d. and the food, etc., expenditure 6s. 8d. per head. The other type of case revealed such instances as a man, wife, and four children spending 21s. 11d. per week in house purchase, leaving only 1s. 7d. per head for food, etc., while others showed that 14s. to 15s. per week was spent on rent and 3s. 4d. to 3s. 8d. per head on food, etc.

Instructional classes were attended on two half-days per week and were compulsory. The subjects offered were Boot repairing, Carpentry, Gardening, First-Aid and Physical Culture. Gardening was the most popular of the classes and it was therefore agreed that the men should have the time equivalent to attendance at the afternoon classes for work on their own gardens and allotments. They gave a guarantee that they would spend their time in this way, and invited the gardening instructor to visit them for inspection, help and advice. Four men who were not in a position to work an individual garden cultivated an allotment jointly.

First-Aid classes soon reached a point where further instruction was not needed, but the two hours allowed for Boot repairing proved to be insufficient. For instance, a man would often keep a child home from school while he took its shoes for repair, and it was therefore desirable to finish them in one period. Carpentry was popular, while the physical training was enjoyed in the cold weather but not during a warm spell. Swimming and Life-saving were introduced in hot weather.

The Instructors were eager to create an atmosphere of friendliness and co-operation, interest and loyalty. This they largely succeeded in doing, and they were unanimous in reporting on the greatly improved spirit of initiative and enterprise shown by the men after a month or two's experience. An example of this was seen in the growing readiness of the men to make suggestions, to elect, and to trust spokesmen on their behalf.

Some evidence of the progressive recovery of physical strength, and the acquirement of skill at work is seen in the steady increase in the quantity of mud and soil removed by excavation.

	MUD		SOIL	SOIL
Week	No. of skips removed	Week	No. of skips removed	Average No. of skips removed per day
1	226	2	150	25
		4	212	35
2	225	6	316	52
		8	293	49
4	267	11	319	53
		12	461	77
5	315	14	452	75
9	317	16	625	104

The operation also involved the clearing out of the brook, the banking and turfing of slopes and the laying of footpaths. Ground surrounding the pool was levelled and adjusted to give a pleasant outlook, and, as in most of Bournville's developments, many existing trees were retained.

I can recall a summer's day when my mother took me to see the men busy at work and I can visualise, in my mind's eye, men pushing small trucks from the excavations along a stretch of rail-track, and then tipping the trucks sideways in order to deposit the cargo of mud and soil. Anyone visiting the Valley Parkway can clearly see the area that was filled in this way. It lies at the eastern end of the pool.

In June 1937 a new flag station was built to commemorate the Coronation of King George VI and Queen Elizabeth, and on Regatta days the flags fluttering in the breeze made a spectacular sight. Sadly, over the years the flag-pole fell into disrepair and with financial restrictions and the present-day fear of vandalism a replacement has not materialised.

During the Second World War the parkway was one of the venues used for Birmingham's 'Holidays-at-Home' scheme. The area of grassland at the junction of Woodbrooke Road and Bournville Lane was used as a 'Barrage Balloon' site, and each night I would watch from my bedroom window at the rear of 8 Selly Oak Road, as the huge silvery balloon rose high above the tree tops. With hindsight I suppose it gave me a sense of security at the time.

In 1945 the Bournville Village Trustees handed over the Yachting Pool and parkway to the City of Birmingham. The passing of time and financial constraints have inevitably led to a deterioration of the site, but it is still well visited, and not only by humans, for many water fowl and birds of different types congregate there throughout the year, the most prevalent being the Canada Geese. They thrive on the abundance of scraps fed to them by young and old alike, and this has led to a drastic escalation of excrement, so much so that many, including myself, consider it a health hazard, particularly to young children who visit the pool.

In 1982 Dame Elizabeth Cadbury School published an interesting booklet which serves as a simple guide to the bird life of the Valley Parkway and it includes illustrations and a short text describing each kind of bird found there. I'm sure a further up-to-date study would prove interesting, the number of Canada Geese has certainly grown in recent years.

Family Religious Life

In the late 1920's my parents, having had a Church of England or Methodist upbringing, attended the Religious Society of Friends' (Quakers) Meeting House. They began by going each week to the evening Meeting which was held on Congregational lines, and then started going to morning Meeting for Worship. After a time they applied for and were accepted into membership. My sister and I were accepted at the same time.

In a previous chapter I referred to a talk my mother gave to the Bournville School PTA, in 1966. She had mentioned a Sunday School taking place in the School buildings. That Sunday school was run on undenominational lines and had been founded by a George Hamilton Archibald. He had been born in Canada and spent much of his youth in Halifax, Nova Scotia. In an account of his life, written by his daughter Ethel Archibald Johnston, we are told that when he was 17 years of age he attended St Andrew's Church in Halifax and the Minister of that Church was instrumental in guiding the young fellow to a career.

> He sometimes told the story of a white-haired man, a saint if ever there was one, who put his hand on his shoulder and said, 'My boy, you are coming to a Sunday School next Sunday and you are going to take a class.' 'No, indeed I am not' replied George. But the minister countered quietly, 'Yes you are' and he did.

Little did that minister know then that George Hamilton Archibald would become the founder of Westhill School, now Westhill College, one of the Selly Oak Colleges, or that he would be asked by George Cadbury to be responsible for the running of a Sunday School in the village. It was George Cadbury's wish that children should have a Sunday School to go to. To him it was important that they should know and learn from the Bible. As the day school buildings were nearing completion in 1906, the artist Sargent Florence was invited to paint frescoes depicting scenes from the Old Testament stories on the walls of the Junior School hall. The foreword to Ethel Archibald Johnston's biography of her father, written by Roderic Dunkerley, sometime Principal of Westhill College, reads:

> I welcome this book chiefly because it renews Dr Archibald's challenge to the Churches to give the children their rightful

place at the heart of things – to value them, to seek to understand them, to meet their great needs, to bind them into the life of the Christian Community, and to love them and serve them for Christ's sake.

My sister and I attended the Sunday School and when I reached 14 years of age I was asked to be a teacher in the primary department.

When Dr Archibald died in 1938, his son-in-law Andrew Johnston became superintendent and when he died, a few years later, my father was asked to become superintendent. He accepted and held that position until the Sunday School closed in the early 50's. My mother had been both a teacher and Cradle Roll secretary of the School for many years and we were all very sad when it had to close down due to dwindling numbers. Some children transferred to the junior church at St Francis and others moved to the Friends' Meeting House where they would spend the first 20 minutes or so in the Meeting for Worship before going to their own classes for religious teaching. As we reached teenage we were expected to stay in the Meeting for the full hour.

Quakers base their Meeting for Worship on silence, sitting quietly in a group waiting for the spirit to move them to speak, offer a prayer or read a piece of literature or poetry, but once the elders have shaken hands to give an outward sign that worship is over, my word how the tongues wag! This was certainly true at Bournville. Meeting ended at noon, then there would be the reading of notices and once a month Meeting for Worship would be followed by a preparative business meeting. The fingers of the clock moved steadily onward and one by one those of us who were to be involved in the Sunday School at 3 p.m. would ask to be excused. There seemed to be precious little time at home before it was time to set out once again.

We were fortunate to have students from Westhill College to help us with class teaching, tho' this only happened during term time and when the Easter holidays came and again in the summer break we found it difficult to arrange a reasonable number of teachers; after all, everyone was entitled to an annual holiday. However we survived. I still see some of my former pupils from time to time and they all without exception consider those were happy days.

As I have already mentioned I attended Sunday School from the age of four and at 14 started to teach the primary age group children. All leaders and teachers were expected to be at 'training class' held at the Meeting House on Friday evening, where we each would study the lesson for the following Sunday. The meeting began with 'Devotional' and we had to take it in turns to introduce that part of the evening. We then split into groups for each department and we would usually finish by 9.30.

In addition to morning service we would attend evening Meeting as well. This was run on congregational lines with an opening hymn, a Bible reading followed by a period of prayer. A collection would be taken up and notices of forthcoming meetings would be read. The evening meeting choir would sing an anthem, with Tom Osborne conducting and Nellie Woodward playing the organ. A speaker, usually a local person, would then give an address. Once or twice a year arrangements would be made for someone from overseas to give an address. We were fortunate in having The Missionary Guest House in College Walk so near and it was from a steady flow of missionaries spending a well earned furlough there that speakers were drawn. There would be a final hymn and benediction. I sang in the choir for several years and thoroughly enjoyed both Thursday night choir practice and the Sunday evening service. I have heard many fine speakers pass on a message of goodwill and hope. Others may not have been so eloquent but they too were sincere in their interpretation of passages from the scriptures.

You may be forgiven for thinking that was Sunday finished with. But not a bit of it. After evening Meeting the younger element, those aged from 14 to 21+ would walk along Linden Road to meet at 'The Lofts' in Bournville Lane, behind The Olde Farm Inn, now Peaches Restaurant. The buildings were once part of Froggatt's Farm and they were used by Adult School, Scouts, and various other organisations including Youth Club. Every Sunday one of our leaders or a member of the group would introduce a subject for discussion. I remember we once had a series on the different types of church and for several Sundays we visited Roman Catholic, Congregational, Methodist and Church of England places of worship.

We also met up for 'club' on Wednesday evenings as well. 'The Lofts' were old buildings, lit by gas-light and heated by antiquated gas fires that had a habit of going pop every so often. One big meeting hall was heated by two coke stoves. During the Second World War it was used as a Friends' Relief Service clothing collection and storage centre and we used to sometimes help with the sorting. I can smell the fumes from the benzine as I write. From what I remember of the piles of jumpers, suits, coats, scarves, and slippers and shoes I imagine many folk must have been grateful for the generosity of their benefactors.

One other thing that springs to mind when I think of 'The Lofts' is that, like the Forth Bridge, decorating was never finished. I seem to remember we applied many gallons of green Walpamur to the walls, and was it white or cream to the ceilings? I know when we left after an evenings work we wondered what it would look like on our next visit. More often than not another coat had to be applied.

We didn't have the distractions of television in those days but we were given many opportunities. The chance to integrate with other folk our own age and to be led by our leaders, who in later life turned out to not be so very much older than ourselves. Their leadership was invaluable and I am grateful to them, each and every one.

My Father's Business

By the year 1930 my father considered starting up his own land-scape gardening business. He felt he had gained sufficient knowledge of buying, pricing and retailing materials needed for providing a gardening service, and this together with an inborn natural flair for design and perspective persuaded him to go it alone. My mother with her usual calmness accepted the challenge of the clerical side of the business and many's the time I have watched her busily typing esti-mates and invoices on the old Bar-Lock typewriter.

Fortunately, at about this time, the Society of Friends at Bull Street in the centre of Birmingham were arranging for the building of larger premises, including a new Meeting House. Their plans were hampered by the existence of burial vaults which made it impossible for contractors to use heavy lorries when retrieving heavy soil and clay from footings, thus preparing the way for new foundations. One Friend on the planning committee was Leonard P. Appleton, who at the time was Secretary of Bournville Village Trust. He knew my father was starting his own business and he approached him to see if he would be willing to undertake the removal of clay and soil. Father's vehicle was an old 8 cwt. Morris van at the time, but with ingenuity he converted it to an 8 cwt. pick up truck by removing two thirds of the roof, leaving just the driving cab enclosed. For several weeks he would be seen driving up and down the Bristol Road from Bull Street to the then fast-developing Frankley Beeches City Council Estate, where he would

Selly Oak Road.
The entrance to
Bournville Park,
1934.

offload and then make the journey back to the city centre. A tedious task which took many man hours to complete, but the resulting payment for a job well done became the financial basis on which a thriving landscape gardening business was to develop.

In those early years father made all his own slabs. He made moulds measuring two feet by one foot from old wooden packing cases. The cement mixture was made up of three parts sand, two of lime and one of cement, with just the correct amount of water for mixing. All this work was done on the terrace in the back garden of our home. Once the concrete had set, the moulds were easily dismantled and reconstructed for the next batch. I still have the small spade I had as a

Father's Flower Show display, 1937.

Exhibit – Weoley Hill Flower Show.

103

present one birthday and it is a reminder of the times when I mixed and shovelled to help the business on its way. It has one or two rough bits on the shaft, but after 60 years it is still put to good use from time to time.

There are several monuments to the work father did in those days and two in particular have altered very little over the years. They are the two triangular shaped low walls at the Hay Green Lane/Selly Oak Road entrance to Bournville park and the bigger walling at the junction of Oak Tree Lane and Linden Road on the northern boundary of the village. These were made in the late autumn of 1934 when my mother was expecting her second child, my sister Janette. The front garden of 4a Selly Oak Road has a short flight of steps and these too were constructed at around about the same time.

For the next four years the business grew and flourished; no job large or small was turned down. Father spent many hours measuring up garden plots and longer time drawing up plans to submit for customers' approval. It would be wrong of me to say he was always successful, but on the whole there were not many enquiries made that resulted in the job going to rival businesses. He employed men to dig, mix concrete, dress and face stone for walling, lay paving slabs, mow lawns, cut hedges. I can picture in my mind's eye the Enfield Motor mower he used on a cricket pitch. The venue eludes me but I do know I was given the task of picking up sticks and debris before the mowing began. My reward? A drink of tea from the billie can.

I have several photographs, including an album of tinted prints, of gardens he designed and constructed. The original photographs were taken by Percy Bott whose studios were at the corner of Linden Road and Franklin Road, Kings Norton. One print shows the photographer's car in the background. Each picture shows that from a small beginning, Edgar Owen, Landscape Gardener, went on to create gardens of many varied designs from places as far afield as Dorridge, Lickey, Kings Norton, Selly Park and all parts in between.

Father had a stock yard at the bottom of Laburnum Road, Bournville, where York paving and walling stone, Westmorland stone, stone from the Cotswolds, and stone from Grinshill in his beloved Shropshire was stacked alongside tons of sand and gravel, cement and ashes. Ashes I recall were fetched from the Birmingham University boiler houses. Sand and gravel were purchased from the Marlbook sand and gravel company. Some goods were delivered by rail as there

Corner of Somerdale and Claines Road.

was a siding which branched off from the main London Midland and Scottish Railway line. Other goods arrived by road. As a child I looked forward to the days when the delivery of York paving was due because the huge lorry would arrive outside our home at about seven-thirty in the morning having been travelling overnight. The drivers usually agreed to me going with them and father to unload the stock. Those, to my mind, huge lorries would be swallowed up by today's juggernauts, but what a thrill it was to be able to climb up into the driver's cab and be transported the short distance involved. I was in another world and the envy of my playmates.

As the business expanded father contacted 'Vinculum', a subsidiary of 'Tarmac', and their representative, a Mr J. L. Cotterell, would call at the family home once a month to take any orders. In addition to paving slabs of varying sizes his firm supplied concrete rabbits, squirrels, owls, birdbaths, and sundials. My sister and I each have an owl and a rabbit from those days and display them in our own gardens to this day. The original brochure advertising such items quotes the purchase price as seven shillings and sixpence each. Mr Cotterell and his wife became very good friends of my parents, and my sister and I spent many happy times with them and their children.

Garden being constructed – Claines Road with Heath Road/Hole Lane beyond.

Another person contacted with regard to garden ornaments was a Mr Ben Charlesworth of Underbank Old Road, Holmfirth, Yorkshire. I have the pictorial post card he sent my father as reply, stating 'Prices on application'. I do not know the outcome, but I wonder, do they still make garden ornaments in Holmfirth?

In the 1930's a huge Flower Show was held on a Saturday each August in the Girls' Recreation Grounds of Cadbury Brothers, Bournville Lane. Marquees were erected and exhibitors would spend many hours staging their produce and displays. For several years father would mount one such in the commercial tent. I well remember having the job of staining many pieces of trellis work.

By 1939 the business had 40 men on the pay roll. Methods of advertising used were many and varied, from a page in the Bournville Council Year Book and Children's Festival Programmes to, briefly, a very short film on the local cinema screen. His last big display was

Show-ground – Collin's Furriers, 1939.

Rear garden – Middle Park Road, Weoley Hill.

made on a piece of land leased from Collins' the furriers in Maryvale Road. The display was actually on a site in Linden Road, in more recent years occupied by a Service Station. Here he laboriously laid out ornamental pools and lawns with rockeries of Westmorland stone, planted with spring flowering bulbs. That was in the late summer and early autumn of 1939. By December the whole area had been transformed to make way for air raid shelters for the employees of the furriers. With that went a large chunk of father's capital. The dark clouds of war were overhead and with them had come the conscription of many of the business's workforce, some to munitions factories, others to serve in H.M. forces. Some did not return. By the spring of 1940, father was left with one lorry, one wheelbarrow, a spade, a fork and a stirrup pump and bucket; everything had been commandeered. He was distraught.

My Days at Bournville School

At the time my parents were building up their business I was a pupil at Bournville School. I well remember the day my mother took me to meet the then headmistress, Miss Greenway, and to be enrolled. We sat in the corridor outside her office until my name was called. She welcomed us both and asked my mother many questions. At one stage she asked us to both sit quietly for a few moments, whereupon the school clock, housed in the junior school building, began to play the chimes for three o'clock. Simultaneously the cuckoo clock in her office announced to the world that it was indeed three o'clock. In later years I was to learn that other intending pupils had remembered a similar enrolment day.

Having been accepted as a pupil I duly started in the September of 1932. My first teacher was a Miss Whitehouse, and there were Miss Davis, Miss D'eath and Miss Powell. What happy days I was to have with my friends and other children of the village. We were all encouraged to give of our best. We were blessed with well-equipped classrooms and the playgrounds were spacious. There was a school garden which we carefully tended and in which we painstakingly planted spring flowering bulbs in the autumn and annual seeds each spring. The small pathways between the flower beds were weeded and kept tidy. The poppies were huge specimens and had to be seen to be believed. Needless to say, with my father being a keen gardener, I was in my element when gardening lessons arrived. To this day I gain immense pleasure and a great sense of well-being after an hour spent tending my plot, even tho' the joints creak and the back aches as a result.

Every year the Children's Festival was held on the Men's Recreation Ground at Cadbury Brothers. During the weeks prior to this, heats of races would be run off in the school playground and on the lawn that lies on the Linden Road side of the school. To my infant eyes that lawn seemed to be the size of a football pitch.

I remember one crisis occurring during my infant school days. It was when I was in Miss Powell's class, top infants I think. Another girl managed to get a piece of her pencil rubber stuck up her nose. There was such a to-do. We all thought she was about to die, and teacher looked a bit faint as well. Eventually a teacher from an adjoining class-room heard the commotion and by some means, tho' I do not remember how, the eraser was extracted and the lesson continued. Recently my daughter has taken up her first teaching appointment and from her experience it would appear that this type of mishap is by no means uncommon, for two children in her class have recently performed in a similar manner, using a small stone or a screw.

Needless to say the term leading up to Christmas was a busy one with many and varied items made for parents; calendars, book-marks, needle cases. The snip snip of scissors was heard, the occasional yelp when someone inadvertently cut themselves instead of the card. One lasting memory I have from those far off days, is of the paste we used. It came in silvery coloured canisters and had a pungent smell of almonds. Towards the end of term a Nativity play would be staged, together with carol singing for children and parents. On the last day we were all provided with a Christmas party tea and each year Dame Elizabeth Cadbury would visit us accompanied by her companion, Elsa Fox, and members of her family.

During Spring and Summer terms we were encouraged to take wild flowers and other nature specimens for decoration of the class-room. The window ledges would be strewn with jam jars full of cow parsley, cowslips, buttercups, meadowsweet and all types of grasses, not forgetting the frogspawn and occasional stickleback. I wonder where all those frogs went to? We grew runner bean plants in gas jars, with the beans placed between a layer of blotting paper and the jar.

With present day ball point and cartridge pens children may not know what blotting paper is, any more than my generation could believe our parents had written their lessons on a slate.

One day, while I was at home having lunch with my family, my father spotted a tiny field mouse scurrying across our garden rockery. I wanted to catch it. To this day I don't know how my father caught it, but catch it he did and placed it in my Mickey Mouse sea-side bucket. He suggested I should take it to show my teacher, so, together with two neighbouring friends, I walked back to school with my quarry. To say teacher was not very well pleased would be an understatement. However, she let all those who wanted to see the mouse before ordering me and my partners in crime to return home and let the poor creature free to roam our rockery once more. Happy carefree days.

By 1937 I had moved up into the junior school where Mr Johnson was headmaster. It was at this stage that the necessity for clear legible writing, the reading of good books and careful spelling together with concentration when it came to arithmetic was made known to be of paramount importance. Up until that time I had managed in my infant way to cope with the basics of the three R's but to me lessons of that nature had been iced with the time spent on craft lessons. Life in the junior school certainly gave one a feeling of superiority over the infants.

I have to thank two members of staff, namely Mr Horsley and Mr Barker (they were two teachers my mother referred to in her talk to the PTA), for teaching me the basics of music, particularly choral singing. Their enthusiasm encouraged me at an early age to not only listen to but to take part in musical activities. I can see, in my mind's eye, Mr Horsley on the stage of the Cadbury Brothers Concert Hall conducting the annual Carol Concert with Mr Clifford Ball playing the organ, and I can hear him booming out the words of the carol 'Unto Us a Boy is Born'. 'Let the organ thunder', and thunder it did. Mr Morley was another enthusiastic chorister and sang regularly in the St Francis Church choir. From time to time he would recruit boys from school for the church choir.

As I progressed, along with others my age, I was expected to write with an ink pen. I often wondered who it was who stuffed the inkwells at the corners of the desks with scrappy bits of blotting paper and scraps of wool thus making it impossible for one to dip one's pen in and extract it without lots of little hairs or bits being on the end, resulting of course in spider-like blobs appearing all over one's clean page of paper. With all these hazards Mr Ward insisted that clear writing was a necessity if one wanted to get on in the world, and how painstakingly he tried to teach us how to write with flowing loops and curves. I also remember he was the teacher who, for several weeks, would read a chapter from *Doctor Dolittle* in last lesson on a Friday. *Wind in the Willows* was another book kept for Friday. You may be forgiven for thinking we only had men teachers, but there were women on the staff as well. There was Miss Hogg. She was the girls' Gym teacher. With the greatest respect she did not have the sylph-like figure of today's 'green goddess', but if she said do a thing you did it or lived to reap the consequences. Miss Farrar taught English and she would produce the annual school play. From time to time the thespians among us would represent school in a drama festival. My only claim to fame in one such was when I provided a knitted duck as a prop, and my grandmother had knitted that. Otherwise, the only time I actually had a speaking part was when I was chosen to be the mirror on the wall in *Snow White and the Seven Dwarfs*, and that happened because I had a voice loud enough to penetrate the stage curtains when asked 'Mirror, mirror on the wall, who is the fairest of them all?'

Mr Clifton taught the sciences and Mr Webb carpentry, the latter being for boys only; girls had to do cookery. I don't recall many science lessons, but whether that is because the subject wasn't taught to pupils at the lower end of the school or because I just didn't take it in is debatable.

In addition to the customary school photographs, including a panoramic one of the whole of the junior school taken in 1938, I do have mementoes of my time at Bournville School. They are two books, *Alice in Wonderland* by Lewis Carroll and *The Wonder Book of Why and What*. Both were presented to me for being the child who collected the greatest amount of money for 'Children's Charities' a forerunner surely of 'Children in Need'.

In March 1939 I sat the entrance examination for George Dixon Secondary School, Edgbaston, and passed, thanks in no small measure to the dedicated teaching staff of Bournville School, and the encouragement and coaching I was given by my teacher uncle Albert Guest. So, one door closed and another opened.

Bournville Park.

Bournville Park – Part 2

I spent many happy hours of my childhood playing with my friends in the Park. We would persuade our parents to let us buy a fishing net from Mr Creed's shop on the Green and that, together with an old jam jar, meant we were equipped to stand for hours on the banks of the brook, patiently waiting for an unsuspecting tiddler to emerge from its stony safe haven to be quickly scooped up in the net and carefully deposited in the already water filled jar; water from the brook of course, tap water was not suitable, it was too clean. The newly opened yachting pool was also a venue for such activity, but occasionally model yacht enthusiasts made we juvenile anglers rather unwelcome. In hindsight I imagine any self-respecting tiddler would keep to the depths when sailing was in progress, so perhaps we benefited from reproach after all.

With the opening of the Valley Parkway and yachting pool many Bournville children wanted a model yacht or clockwork speed-boat when a birthday was due. Many many times children have gone home to bed leaving father or older brother to wait until a reluctant yacht edged its way to the shore, having been stranded in the middle of the pool by a lull in the wind. At one time, the boat-house keeper would don his long waders and go out into the middle of the pool to retrieve a becalmed boat.

Springtime would see our quarry change to frog-spawn, easier to locate but a slimy messy job to catch. I wonder how many jam jars of the stuff have stood on the window ledges of schools through the ages? I have to admit to being interested in monitoring the development of tadpoles, but please don't mention frogs in my presence, for they make me feel positively ill. Why? I do not know. All I know is they are definitely out as far as I am concerned, even tho' I hear gardeners singing their praises.

During the 1930's and 40's I remember there was a small wooden hut standing alongside the park-keeper's shed. It was Mr and Mrs Summers' sweet shop, and what a 'child-gatherer' that was when it opened on a Saturday and Sunday afternoon. Not only children flocked to it to purchase aniseed balls, and liquorice laces, soda and lime lollipops, Blue-bird toffee, and ice cream cornets and wafers – to mention just a handful of delights – but the adults who played bowls and tennis, together with those just visiting, were able to order a tray with cups, saucers, and plates with a pot of tea, milk, sugar and buttered bread (with or without preserve) and assorted biscuits or cakes. I can visualise Mrs Summers and her daughters serving customers whilst working in what must have been very uncomfortable conditions, because I'm sure the kettle boiled continually on an anthracite stove with the shortest flue, and the hut itself was quite small, maybe 10ft. by 8 ft. with a pitched roof, and we did get really hot summer days. Yes, such people deserved every penny they earned. As for their lock-up shop, would that we could have such things today without the fear of vandalism.

As a child I would often take a peep inside the park-keeper's shed and gaze at the neat rows of well used and perfectly cared for shovels, spades, forks, edging shears and hoes. The hay-rake which hung from the roof and wasn't just used for gathering hay but to retrieve a wayward tennis ball that had found its way to the brook. How beautiful the whole place was kept and with such tender loving care by the head keeper and his men. Even as I write I can picture the scene and smell the aroma of the anthracite stove and the creosoted wooden building as the fumes waft to the sky.

What other activities did we children get up to? There was the usual football and cricket, french cricket, tennis, skipping, hop-scotch, hide and seek, cops and robbers, cowboys and Indians. Those who dared would wear wellington boots, or more likely, remove shoes and socks to wade in the brook and gather large stones and rocks, bits of branches that had broken from overhanging trees and gradually build up a dam. At the end of the day the big question would be, 'will it still be here tomorrow?'.

Can you remember, is it cow parsley that has small nodules on its roots? If so that was the plant we would search out during the summer months and more often than not one of the boys would have a Scout knife, or maybe mother had been cajoled into loaning an old kitchen knife: either way we children would dig below the plant to retrieve the said nodules. Nowadays such goings on would not be allowed because of conservation, but 60 years ago we were oblivious of such matters and a freshly dug handful of 'pig-nuts', wiped clean with a handkerchief, went down a treat, as did the new leaves of hawthorn (referred to as bread and cheese).

They were happy carefree days and even tho' our parents must have been aware of the threat of war, we played whenever the opportunity arose and we did have fun.

Second World War – Part 1

The first day at my new school was Thursday 31st August 1939. When I arrived there, the school buildings seemed to be enormous and the sea of unknown faces of both pupils and teaching staff together with a certain air of hustle and bustle, meant I inevitably suffered the dreadful butterflies. What I did not understand at the time was that there was far worse to come, for that first day at Secondary School was to be the only full day I actually attended the City Road site for some months to come, because Friday the 1st September saw a mass exodus of children from Birmingham – infant, junior and senior age groups, for destinations all over the country.

On that Friday I assembled at school, together with other pupils, to await the arrival of City of Birmingham buses to transport us to the railway station at Five Ways, where, once we arrived, we were ushered into regimented lines to march on to the platform to await one of what I now believe must have been many hundreds of trains deployed for 'the evacuation'. I recall the day as being chilly to start with but as the day progressed it grew steadily warmer. This was accentuated by the fact that as it was autumn term we had been instructed to wear our winter uniform! There we were clad in gym'-slip and blouse, lisle stockings, lace-up shoes, gaberdine raincoat, velour hat, suitably adorned with the red and green hat band of the school colours. In addition we had to carry a small suitcase, pump bag, and of course the newly acquired cardboard box containing a gas mask. I have very vivid memories of that scene at Five Ways station. I remember how one poor girl was unfortunate enough to get her fingers trapped in the carriage door, and I often wonder whether she would have cried quite as much if it hadn't been for the fact she was leaving home and loved ones behind.

The actual train journey to my destination, Gloucester, was to me uneventful. From time to time the smuts from the funnel of the engine would blow in through the open carriage windows, and hot sticky hands wiped little wan faces. Before long we became very grubby. Eventually our train drew into Gloucester station. From there we were taken to a kind of community hall and were put on display so that intending 'foster parents' could take their pick. That is the impression I had at the time and it has remained with me all through the years. After a while a woman from Linden Road, Gloucester, decided I would do and together with a girl from the Handsworth area of Birmingham, I was led to my new home. We passed allotments and a weather station on the way, and we had to use a footbridge over railway lines. I was very tired when we eventually arrived at 182 Linden Road, tired and very emotional. I confess I slept fitfully that night.

The next day was a Saturday and I spent the whole day with my new family and my fellow evacuee. My foster parents had a four-year-old daughter and I imagine she was very bewildered by having two complete strangers suddenly taken into her home. I was very homesick, maybe because I had left my four-year-old sister at home.

When Sunday 3rd September dawned, and with it the now historical announcement from Prime Minister Neville Chamberlain that Great Britain was at war with Germany, I think the reality of what the previous few days had been leading up to suddenly became abundantly clear. For everyone, young and old, male and female, emotions could be suppressed no longer; we sat and cried quite openly. Strangely, that night, I slept like a log.

I have memories of feeling unwanted by my foster parents, and remember I felt more at ease and happier with a family on the other side of the road. It took me a long time to come to terms with having to have a dripping cake for breakfast, and more difficult still to have to take it in turns to be the one to go to actually buy the newly baked dripping cakes from the corner shop.

The girls and staff of Ribston Hall Girls' School afforded us a wonderful welcome. In recent years I have realised just how disruptive to the day-to-day running of their school our intrusion must have been. We took it in turns to use the school premises. They would have morning lessons in school and we would attend in the afternoon. At other times church halls and community centres were the venues for lessons. Our PE and games lessons were held at the Wagon Repair Works Sports ground on Tuffley Road.

Three weeks after arriving in Gloucester I developed mumps, which wasn't really surprising because my sister had been suffering from the same illness when I left Birmingham. I was admitted to the Over Isolation Hospital for three weeks because I was living in a house where there were other children. I have often wondered why it was the then Chief Medical Officer for Birmingham had told my mother it would be all right for me to be evacuated. During my spell in hospital, teachers and friends kept in touch by writing to me and Miss Ella Ritchie, George Dixon School's headmistress visited me regularly. I count the day she arrived with fruit and several copies of *Picturegoer* a red letter day. I had expected school text books!

I know many of my school chums fared better than I in their particular foster homes, but I do not condemn my 'Gloucester mother and father' for my unhappiness, for I must have had faults, and perhaps if I had been a little older I would have found it easier to adapt to the events of the time.

In recent years we have recalled the outbreak of the Second World War and I have been led to think of the many millions of people of all colours and creeds who today find themselves suffering the ravages of war, their homes and families destroyed by man's inhumanity to man. Indeed in some countries of the world there are children who are the age I was, and older, when the Second World War started who have never known what it is like to live in peaceful surroundings.

I have only visited Gloucester once since 1939, and then only briefly finding time to picnic on 'Robin's Wood Hill' on my way back from a family holiday in Devon. My son and daughter refer to that day as 'Mom's history lesson of war-time experiences'. Perhaps one day I might feel inclined to re-acquaint myself with the place and its people, and remember to say a big 'Thank you' for the brief time I was an adopted daughter.

Towards the end of 1939 arrangements were made for those who wanted to return home for Christmas. I was fortunate because my father came in his lorry to collect me and my companion from Handsworth. The day we travelled was bitterly cold and frosty and as we approached Brosmgrove, travelling along the A38, it began to snow. The rest of the journey was made in blizzard conditions and coming over the Lickeys was really quite treacherous. Once home, I was to remain there for the duration of the war.

My grandmother had moved to live with my parents about the time I was evacuated and years later I was told that my sister had been convinced that my evacuation and the war had all been due to her making the move.

Those years were very difficult for everyone, particularly adults who were aware of what was going on. For a short time my father was out of work; no one thought of having garden landscaping done, and anyway materials were in short supply, and such work was not considered essential, so he was in a dilemma. He spent many hours wondering how to earn a living. He had always been used to working out of doors and the thought of having to work in a factory horrified him. From stories told I understand that one day in October he was sat in very pensive mood when my mother asked him to get some wood for the fire. This was a turning point. He decided there and then to concentrate on building up a firewood and logs business. In those days everyone had an open fire and it being wartime coal and coke were in short supply, so he went ahead with confidence. He was able to rent a stock yard in Old Barn Road at the time and it was there that he set to and built two sizeable sheds that were to house the chopping benches and bundling machines. A smaller open-ended construction housed a circular saw. He had three bundling machines and several axes and choppers and claw hammers of various sizes. For a time the bundles of wood were secured with wire, similar to today's floristry wire, but after a very short time this was unavailable, so an alternative had to be found. One thing did seem to be in fairly plentiful supply and that was tyre inner tubes. My mother, father and I spent many winter evenings cutting rubber bands from such tubes, and what blisters we got as a result! The shears we used were really quite heavy and cumbersome, but they did the trick and the resulting bands were duly put to use. Customers were asked to return them if possible in case the supply suddenly ran out. For the duration of the war, whenever we had a spare moment we would go to the stockyard and chop and bundle wood and put up sacksful of 50 at a time. As luck would have it a ready market was available. Local newsagents and ironmongers were used as the middle man.

Many of the folk who had employed father as a landscape gardener formed a nucleus of customers for his new business. As I grew older I occasionally would go with a lorry driver to a wood at Frankley (the site of present day Frogmill Estate), and help him to load cord wood father had purchased from the landowner. All this after school and homework had been done. Each night we would go to bed wondering whether there would be an air raid. If we did hear the sirens we would make our way to the air-raid shelter father had built in the back garden, while he would have to go to the stock yard because of the risk of fire. Sometimes he would get 10 minutes' walk away when the all clear would sound. The air-raid shelter accommodated a neighbour and her two sons as well as my mother, grandmother, sister and me. I don't remember the neighbour's husband actually sleeping in the shelter, and with hindsight I imagine he would either be at work or else firewatching or ARP duty. In addition to the shelter in the garden we also had a Morrison table shelter which served as a table but was able to sleep two or three people beneath it. It was housed in the sitting room. In 1940 Bournville had a raid which lasted 13 hours, during which time a bomb fell through the bridge which carries the canal and railway over Bournville Lane, adjacent to Bournville Station. As a consequence part of Bournville Lane and a sizeable area of the Cadbury factory was flooded. I recall the railway was not damaged.

They were frightening times but we children would very often spend our spare time walking or cycling around the locality collecting pieces of shrapnel that had splintered into all kinds of shapes. On one such venture in 1940 we came across barriers at the corner of Cob Lane and Griffins Brook Lane and could see a huge crater in the field opposite. That spot is now marked by the Serbian Orthodox Church, and as I write I am aware of the atrocities that are being perpetrated today, 50 years on, in what was Yugoslavia.

Another heavy air raid occurred during the Easter holidays in 1941 and reports tell us that Bournville Junior School was opened as a Rest Centre for over 20 people. I imagine that was as the result of four houses in Hawthorne Road, nos. 12–18, and four in Bournville Lane, nos. 225–231 being destroyed or seriously damaged.

In August 1944 the School was again opened as a Rest Centre. On that occasion it received mothers and young children who had been evacuated from London and the South East to flee flying bomb attacks. I remember my parents found room for a Spanish woman and her small son. Her command of the English language amounted to several superlatives of which I, until that day, had been unaware. While all this was going on around us we were aware that others not so far from Bournville were having a far more horrendous time.

My sister and I, together with our playmates, attended school as though nothing untoward was happening. Many times, when travelling on the no. 11 bus to school in City Road, I would have to go to a public air raid shelter because the sirens had sounded, usually because a German bomber making a last-minute dash for home, had lost his bearings and was likely to pepper the street with machine-gun fire. I don't know why but this type of occurrence would usually take place as we approached the junction of Harborne Lane and Metchley Lane, Harborne. Once the all clear was given we went on our way once more.

One of the saddest times of my school life was on the day I arrived at school to find that several houses opposite were laid flat or severely damaged and were heaps of rubble. The school itself had been hit with incendiary bombs which resulted in a severe fire. The ground floor was awash with water left from the firefighting hoses. We were all paddling about on duck boards doing our best to salvage as much as possible in the way of books, stationery and furniture. The staff who had been firewatching during the night looked absolutely worn out. That was the day the headmistress announced that some members of school had been killed, and I learned what it was like to lose someone I knew, as a result of war.

My days at George Dixon were happy ones. I was not a particularly good scholar and was called upon to sign the Excellent Book rarely. My signature is more likely to be found in the Order Book or detention files. In my final year I did gain a games badge for my contribution to the school rounders team. I played in the school hockey team as well but never gained a badge for my efforts. I enjoyed tending the form garden and would have loved to go on to Horticultural College, but with my reluctance to be conscientious and study for exams my expectations were dashed.

Writing of school days has reminded me of the journeys made by tram-car from Five Ways to Kent Street Baths for swimming instruction, and of the organised visits to matinee performances of *The Rivals* and *She Stoops to Conquer* at the Old Repertory Theatre.

I am also reminded of two school friends who, together with their parents, spent many hours painstakingly painting sea shells and, when the paint had dried, would mount the shells, carefully grading them by size, on to a length of silk rope, the result being an acceptable necklace. (My aunt Amy, her husband and family made similar items with carefully sand-papered beech nut case, again painted in a variety of colours and joined together with floristry wire. Six or seven bound together made a delightful buttonhole brooch.) Times were hard but life went on.

Second World War – Part 2

For 18 months, or thereabouts, I worked in the gardens and greenhouses of the Manor House on Saturday mornings and during the school holidays. Mr Mason was head gardener and he had several men working under him. I recall a Mr Mole, Mr Gibbs, Mr Beaver and Mr Cheal. The hothouses were well stocked with exotic plants from warmer climes and in the summer months the crop of tomatoes produced was phenomenal. There was a resident parrot who squawked and chattered continually. Mr Mole was in charge of the greenhouses and many times I heard the parrot say 'the old lady's coming'. He had, of course, heard this uttered many times by gardeners when giving warning of Dame Elizabeth Cadbury's approach. She was a gracious lady and when she heard the parrot herself, would take it all in good fun.

The ornamental and kitchen gardens together with the surrounding grounds and lake were a joy to behold. The recent showing of *A Victorian Kitchen* on BBC Television, tho' of an earlier period of time, has evoked many happy memories for me.

I have weeded rockeries, edged lawns, cut long grass with a sickle, and bear a scar to prove it; picked peaches, pears, plums, and apples, helped to tray them and stack them in the store-houses. Once or twice I helped three men to sweep the long drive of leaves. It took the whole of a Saturday morning, and we started at 7.30a.m. I remember how proud I was when I had my first pay-packet. It contained 10/6d. and with that money I bought a long-awaited stamp album which I still have today.

Others have written at length about the Manor House and grounds. I must say how very much I enjoyed those days. Dame

Elizabeth Cadbury and her companion, Elsa Fox, the housekeeper, cooks, chauffeur (dear Tutton), the gardeners, Mr Prentice the man in charge of Manor Farm, all made me feel welcome and I am grateful for the times I spent in their company.

Manor Park, now in the hands of Birmingham City Parks Department, has, in recent times been scheduled as a site of importance for nature conservation.

During the war, Bournville land awaiting development, i.e. the now Shenley and Lower Shenley Estates, was not allowed to go to waste but instead was let to farmers, and the existing agricultural buildings and fences were maintained in good condition. Shendley Court Farm, Yew Tree Farm and Upper Shendley Fields Farm and Middle Park Farm were managed by a Land Agent. A great deal of the land at Rowheath and in various parkways was also handed over for the cultivation of cereal crops.

The barn and other buildings at Manor Farm were adapted for use by the Friends' Ambulance Unit as a training camp. More than 1,000 young men passed through it during the war years and by 1946 had seen service in many countries of the world. When the war ended and the FAU vacated the place, Birmingham Young Friends (Quakers) and others held many weekend and summer camps there and from experience I can say they were very happy times; and yes, I did go boating on the Manor Lake in the very early hours one summer morning!

The Bournville Village Council Year Book for 1939 reports the Council as having taken an active interest in air raid precautions, having arranged a Public Meeting at the Schools on Wednesday 13th April 1938, and approached the Chief Air Warden with a view to arranging a first aid post and other precautions at Bournville in case of emergency. By 1940 we learn that many approaches had been made to the Council concerning ARP and many wardens had joined for service. The report also states that

> owing to the present national situation Council find it impossible to publish the *Bournville Year Book* in its usual size; the cost of printing materials makes the publication almost prohibitive; but it is hoped that in its reduced size much useful information may be retained.

In June 1940 a branch of the Citizens' Advice Bureau was opened at Ruskin Hall and enquiries could be made between 3 p.m. and 4 p.m.

on a Wednesday. Because of varying restrictions the *Year Book* was not published again until 1948 and the Children's Festival was also cancelled for the duration of the war, starting up again in 1946. Another indication of restrictions is shown in the Printer's advertisement. It reads:

> Specialists in the production of House and Club,
> Monthly, Quarterly, and Yearly publications
> within the limits of paper control.

One place that did remain open throughout the war, tho' at a financial loss, was the Social Centre as it was felt essential for the relaxation of members.

When, eventually, the *Year Book* was published once again, the report of the Village Council read as follows.

> The Village Council has much pleasure in presenting the Year Book for 1948. The book has not been published since 1941. Since that time we have been engaged in a terrible war. Some who live amongst us have lost their loved ones, and we are deeply sorry for them. We hope we shall never see such a calamity again.
>
> During the war your Council carried on with such social service as we were capable of. The Citizens' Advice Bureau was opened at the Ruskin Hall, to give advice and to answer any questions that would give help to those persons who were in need of assistance. This duty was well worth while, and the Council are grateful to the people who came along to help them in this important work. Bournville suffered little as regards air raids. We are happy to report that the houses destroyed by enemy action in Bournville Lane have been re-built and those in Hawthorne Road are at present being re-built.
>
> The Children's Festival was revived again in 1946, and very successful it was, with a good crowd supporting it.
>
> We must place on record the honour paid to one of our neighbours Alderman Albert Bradbeer on being elected to the high office of Lord Mayor of the City of Birmingham.
>
> We congratulate Dame Elizabeth Cadbury on reaching her 90th birthday.
>
> You will observe that new houses are being erected in various parts of the Estate.

The last remark was a sure indication that the war was over and things were beginning to get back to normal.

My Employment

In June 1944 I applied for a job in the offices of Cadbury Brothers, and was fortunate to pass. I commenced work there, in the General Office, on the 28th August of that year. By this time my sister was coming to the end of her junior schooling and was preparing to go to grammar school. When the time came she was successful in gaining a place at Kings Norton Girls School.

The part of my life I spent working at Cadbury Brothers was happy. In those days the firm had their own Education Department, and every employee under the age of 18 was expected to attend Bournville Day Continuation School on one day each week. I used to go on Tuesdays. The usual subjects were studied, English and maths, PE, music, geography, history, but in addition we had Current Affairs, a subject I found fascinating due, in no small part, to the teacher who made the lessons so interesting. I also spent two lesson periods at the Ruskin Hall School of Art where I learned the rudiments of metalwork. I enjoyed the subject so much that I arranged to attend night school for several years and, among other things, I designed and made a silver plated sugar bowl for my parents' Silver Wedding in 1949. Some years later I made an oak bedside cabinet at evening woodwork class and I still use that piece of DIY to this day. The plywood backing still needs staining!

My first placement as I have already said was in the General Office, the department where all things relating to the accounting and invoicing of chocolate and cocoa sales, and customer queries were dealt with. In those days although most invoices were prepared and typed, some were still being handwritten by clerks. Their copper-plate writing in the ledgers had to be seen to be appreciated. Being one of five or six intake into the office I was soon taught the job of office junior. Before long I was allowed to deliver post to other departments within the offices and in some cases had to walk through the factory areas. However, some were out of bounds, but one manufacturing room we were allowed to walk through, as it shortened our journey, was the biscuit covering plant. I soon found out that the biscuits carefully laid out at the end of the enrobing machine were in fact mishapes and were there for the taking. After a few weeks the thought of any more chocolate was nauseating.

I was fortunate in being given the opportunity to learn how to operate both an addressograph machine and a comptometer, and for several months I either addressed or worked out the figure work for invoices. All this was happening as the war was coming to an end.

Invoicing, as I have said, was being done in the way it had been done day in day out since the early part of the century. Before long all that was to change. As men and women drifted back from HM forces, after the declaration of victory in Europe and a little later in Japan, the introduction of modern electronic machinery took place. Hollerith and its punch-card system was the first and presumably one of the forerunners to today's computers. Those machines made it possible for cards to be punched with holes, similar to those on a pianola roll, but instead of picking up hammers of a piano, when placed in a huge printing machine they would activate printing keys and print letters and figures. An invoice would be placed in a roller similar to a typewriter roller and at a press of a button, hey presto! a fully typed invoice would emerge. Those early days saw many hours lost through the teething problems of the machines. I believe the machines were leased to Cadbury's and only electricians employed by Hollerith were allowed to make any repairs or adjustments when things went wrong. This resulted in a great deal of time being wasted with a machine out of order. Frustrating times for senior staff, and operators alike.

I was concerned that machines were taking over and the once fairly quiet office was becoming noisier and noisier by the day. As a result I became unhappy and depressed. After a while I asked for a transfer to another office. My application was accepted and I moved to Service and Training Office in 1951.

As the name implies this was where any task not covered by other offices was done, for instance whenever there was a change in the price of Cadbury goods, it was 'Service and Training' staff who undertook the mammoth task of despatching letters and advertising material giving details of any alterations to all Cadbury customers. In addition to the size of the task there was also the added hurdle of having to get everything ready for despatch by a fixed date. There were approximately 240,000 retail outlets served by Cadbury at the time, and sometimes there would be seven or eight different items to put into each individual envelope. It goes without saying, extra staff were recruited at such times.

In addition to this type of work, the office management were also responsible for the training of new junior office clerks. There would be intakes of school leavers each January, Easter-time and during the summer months. They would have passed an entrance examination and a period of a fortnight in the office, being taught basic office skills, filing in alphabetical and numerical order, etc. would follow. All work was checked and records kept of individual performance. They would also be given talks by senior members of management from office and factory on the running of their particular department. Progress was carefully monitored and at the end of training, clerks would be allocated to the office considered appropriate for their own individual skills.

I was involved with the day-to-day running of the overseas gift scheme. This was closely linked to the Export office and any letters I wrote were signed by a senior member of the Export staff. The job itself entailed the daily collection and recording of orders received from the firm's agents abroad, the typing of invoices giving details of the agent's name, customer's name, item ordered and the address of the recipient. The selection of goods offered varied from a pound box of assorted chocolates to the larger more ornate selection boxes, together with tins of biscuits of varying shapes and sizes. Costs were minimal to quite costly. For eight months of the year from the end of February to September the job was undertaken by me on my own. However when October arrived the orders from Singapore, Kenya, India, USA, Canada, Venezuela, and many other countries, would increase so drastically that arrangements had to be made for temporary seasonal staff to be employed, and typists from other offices would be called upon to work overtime for us to ensure that as many of the orders as possible were despatched in time for delivery at Christmas. Literally hundreds of thousands of boxes of chocolate biscuits would arrive at homes in this country from loved ones working or residing abroad. Not all gifts arrived in time for Christmas but we did our best, we could do no more. We all welcomed the festive break. In the early days of the new year stray orders would continue to arrive, but the bulk of the rush was over. It was then that we would start to receive parcels returned by the GPO marked 'gone away', 'not known at this address', etc., etc. Other returns would be parcels that had been damaged in transit. In those cases a replacement would be despatched. I enjoyed the challenge of that job and regard the eight years spent in that office as among some of the happiest of my life.

During my employ with Cadbury Brothers I took advantage of the many facilities provided for freetime activities. In those days the firm had a very comprehensive library. There were billiard and snooker rooms for the menfolk, in addition to Men's, Youths' and Girls' Recreation and Athletic Clubs. Men's and women's swimming baths with shower facilities; an excellent Dramatic Society and a Musical Society made up of Male Voice Choir, Grand Opera section, Light Opera section and Orchestra and Silver Band.

I enrolled as a member of the girls' athletic club within a week of starting work and was to take part in tennis, hockey, cricket, and the occasional game of squash, both in inter-departmental matches and in teams representing Cadbury. I was privileged to be invited to have lunch with the visiting New Zealand ladies' cricket team when they visited Bournville in the 50's.

My love of music, nurtured from my early days at school, drew me to the chorus of the Grand Opera section and for two or three years I served as Honorary secretary to that body, until I left work to be married in 1959.

Jubilee of Bournville Village Trust

The Jubilee of the Trust should have been held in 1950, but was postponed until 1951 so that it might coincide with the 'Festival of Britain' celebrations.

Bournville's week-long festivities began on Sunday 24th June with an open-air Service on the Green, and ended with the Children's Festival on Saturday 30th June.

An exhibition aimed at reminding older residents of days gone by, and pointing out to the younger members of the community the heritage and values which helped to create Bournville, was held at Minworth Greaves. In its early years the Village did provide a concrete example of what could be done by good housing and planning.

The 1952/53 edition of the *Bournville Village Council Year Book* includes the following.

It is not unnatural that over a period of 50 years the original conception of the Founder should have been altered somewhat, and it may be asked what is the future of the Trust now that conditions are so different from when it was founded. However, the Trust has a duty to manage its existing properties as well as possible in accordance with the ideals of the Founder and the Estate should be a community, not just a group of buildings.

The article goes on to claim,

> . . . it would be wrong for any organisation which has vacant land at the present time not to build houses, and this must be the function of the Trust for many years to come. Whether or not the Trust is still in being to celebrate its centenary, it should at any rate enter its second half-century with principles as real and vital as when it was originally set up by the Founder.

The same publication refers to the death of Dame Elizabeth Cadbury on 4th December 1951, and reminds us that we would do well to remember what the Estate owes to her. As the wife and co-Trustee of the Founder she became Chairman of the Trust when her husband died in 1922, and under her guidance the wishes of the Founder were faithfully carried on and extended. She was deeply interested in anything and everything appertaining to the Trust, in particular the provision of houses for young families, and proper community facilities for those who came to live on the Estate, and in particular the well-being and happiness of the children in the schools.

Upon her death, her eldest son, Laurence Cadbury, became Chairman of Trustees.

Dame Elizabeth Hall

In 1951 there were calls for a Community Centre to be provided for the Bournville Village. There was already a Social Centre in Laurel Grove, but this was considered outdated and no longer catered for the social needs of the residents. Tho' fully aware of the need for such a building it was not possible to proceed with such a project owing to the economic conditions of the time. However the matter would be kept in mind.

By 1958/59 it is reported the Bournville Village Trust moved their offices from Bournville Lane (opposite Main Street) to new premises in Oak Tree Lane, the site of the present Head Offices of the Trust. At the same time it also took over a large building at the rear of the offices, which contained a hall and two smaller rooms. The Trustees and the Trustees of the George Cadbury Fund decided to re-furbish this building as a Community Centre, and that it should be known as Dame Elizabeth Hall in memory of Dame Elizabeth Cadbury.

The Hall was completely re-decorated and re-furnished and a small kitchen provided, and was available for letting. The rooms were suitable for committees or small meetings, and the Hall could be conveniently used for larger meetings, entertainments, 21st birthday parties, wedding receptions and the like. Before long people were taking advantage of the facilities provided for them and from small beginnings the Centre has become a very well-used venue. How pleased Dame Elizabeth Cadbury would be!

Development to the West of Bournville

By the mid-50's the land at Yew Tree Farm to the north west of Bournville had several houses already built on it and Lower Shenley Farm land was beginning to be developed, with 103 dwellings planned for the first phase. They were to be let to families nominated by the City Council. The Trust reports for 1954 state:

> The older Bournville Association can help the new residents to build a full and satisfying community life, and the Trustees commend the idea to the Village Council and Residents' Associations as they look forward and make plans for the year ahead.

SHENLEY COURT RESIDENTS' ASSOCIATION was formed in 1952 and one of its first main objectives was to provide a hall where the residents could meet and socialise. The Bournville Village Trust generously provided materials for the structure, and the hall was built by the residents themselves in their spare time at week-ends, in 1953. It took five months to complete and furnish.

One of the first ventures after the official opening was the setting up of a Sunday School. This was held every week and catered for children between the ages of four and seven years of age.

The ladies of the neighbourhood formed their own guild and held meetings each Wednesday evening and whist drives were held on Thursday evenings during the winter months.

The present Community Centre is situated in Hawkestone Road near the corner of Green Meadow and Clover Roads.

View of Shenley Estate taken from Bristol Road, March 1995.

In addition to these weekly activities other annual events were established, including a Flower and Vegetable Show, garden competitions, and Christmas parties for all the children of the Estate between the ages of four and 15 years. It is reported that approximately 270 to 300 children attended one of the three parties given each Christmas.

My mother's sister Amy Slater and her family were active members of the community with my aunt playing the piano for the Sunday School and my cousins Robert and Gordon Slater helping with the leadership of the Youth Group and the arranging of parties.

By 1960 it was reported that:

> In co-operation with the City of Birmingham 500 houses are being built for allocation to persons from the Corporation Housing list. In addition, five self-build Housing Societies have erected over 100 houses on the Estate.

The writer goes on to say:

129

Shenley Shopping Centre, March 1995.

To an increasing extent, the Estate is achieving importance as a controlled experiment in town-development comparable to a New Town.

By concentrating on the provision of houses of different values for all classes of the community and houses which are of a good standard of design, by assisting in the development of community life, by generous provision of parks and playing-fields, by careful landscaping, and by a reasonable standard of maintenance, the Trustees believe that they are creating something of value.

LOWER SHENLEY RESIDENTS' ASSOCIATION was formed in 1955 and its aims were very similar to those of the Shenley Court Residents' Association, in that they wished to promote the well-being of all children on the Estate, to create good neighbourliness and friendship within the community and to offer facilities for recreational activities to all age groups. The Community Hall, was built, at the back of Burdock Road off Shenley Lane, by men of the Association, with building

Father at work in rear gardens of Green Meadow Road.

materials once again being generously provided by the Bournville Village Trust. The Hall was officially opened by the then Lord Mayor of Birmingham, Donald Johnstone, JP, on March 7th 1959.

So it is evident that as the tentacles of the Village reached out to the limits of Bournville land and joined up with the surrounding City Council Estates of Northfield and Weoley Castle, the aims of the Founder were continually being implemented by the creation of mixed communities, that is, ones in which families of different income levels were able to live together, and by and large this policy achieved success.

I Meet and Marry Leonard Broomfield

When my family moved from Selly Oak Road to 102 Linden Road in 1949 my mother began to purchase the weekly groceries from Bournville Village Stores on the Village Green. By this time more and more people had grown accustomed to buying their weekly groceries, meat and vegetables, a week at a time, unlike our grandparents who bought one or two items only when the necessity arose and the money was available. I'm sure this change in shopping custom came about as the result of war-time rationing, when few commodities were on the shelves and the weight of goods purchased was not too much for carrying.

As things gradually returned to normal after the war, the shopper found more variety of goods in the shops from which to choose purchases and could also buy in greater quantity. It became practical to shop once a week, particularly among those women who were working mothers.

At times it was my duty to drop the grocery order into the Village Stores on my way back to work at mid-day on a Friday. It would then be assembled and delivered the same evening. On one such Friday in March 1958 I found the proprietor, Leonard Broomfield, in quite a flustered state and his attitude struck me as rather unusual, so much so that I asked what troubled him. His reply told me he was dreading the week-end as he had to do stock-taking. I had no idea what a mammoth task lay ahead of him, as I, like many other customers, just saw the goods displayed on the shop shelves, and could not envisage the counting of said goods being a frightening prospect. I remember saying in a fit of complete ignorance, 'Well if I can help in any way, let me know.' His quick response was 'Do you mean that?' 'Of course.' I replied. So it was that along with the shop staff, in those days numbering five or six, I found myself counting and recording endless jars of preserves, tins of fruit, cartons of breakfast cereal, packs of soap and all the other commodities found in a retail grocery store, working from the time the shop closed at 1 o'clock on the Saturday until quite late that evening and again for most of the Sunday.

The whole experience was an eye-opener to me for apart from the actual stock-taking I also found out how large the premises were. Immediately below the shop floor, the area of which had been extended a few years earlier, was a cellar, which housed racks of tinned goods, meats, fish, fruit, condensed milk, and endless jars of preserves of every variety, jams, honey, pickled onions, pickled beetroot, pickled gherkins. One corner was taken up by the cold-store. This was where sides of bacon and hams were hung and tins of corned beef, spam, ham, tongue were stacked alongside cartons of packs of margarine and wooden barrels containing Danish tub-butter.

Bournville Village Stores.

At the rear of the premises there were buildings which, when originally built, catered for the proprietor's pony and trap. There was a stable, complete with manger, and rings fitted in the wall where the tack had hung. The part used for garaging a car or van in the 50's was very lofty and, I was told, had been built that way in order to accommodate the shafts of the trap. Above the garage was a hay loft, complete with pulley.

All these out-buildings were utilised to store stock. The stable contained all the bottled goods; soft drinks such as 'Corona', 'Tizer', soda-syphons. The small room next to the garage contained soaps and soap powders of every variety together with fire-lighters and bundles of fire-wood, the whole giving off an aroma which always reminded me of the little country store where my paternal grandmother had worked during the war. Running across the top of the soap-store and garage was the area where huge boxes containing cartons of breakfast cereal and biscuits were kept. Pre-packed goods were only just beginning to come on the market, so biscuits were dispensed and weighed from a glass-topped tin into a paper bag, a ½lb. or 1lb. at a time.

Finally, the small room at the furthermost end of the outbuildings was where all the sugars were stored, granulated, dark and soft brown, icing, caster, cube – all were found there.

When I saw the amount of goods stored I came to realise just what a huge task stock-taking was. However, by early Sunday evening almost everything had been counted and recorded and with a certain feeling of satisfaction and remuneration, plus a box of Rowntree's Black Magic chocolates I left for home.

A few evenings later I received a 'phone call from Leonard asking if I could help with the calculation and writing up of figures required for the final statement that was to be forwarded to his accountant. I was able to say yes, and as a result I spent many ensuing evenings laboriously tapping away and pen-pushing until everything was completed in time for the previously arranged appointment with the accountant. Stock-taking was completed.

A few weeks later, Leonard, who incidentally had been widowed a few years earlier, invited me to spend an evening at the theatre with him and from that time on our friendship grew and we spent more and more time together. At this time, his daughter, Peggy, was away at the Friends' School, Sidcot in Somerset. It was when she was home for the annual summer vacation that I began to get to know a little about her and the interests she had. I would have Sunday lunch with her and her father and my mother invited them both to meals at our home. In the ensuing weeks Leonard's sister Winifred Burtt and her husband, Eric Burtt, gave me a very warm welcome to their home. (Eric and his brother Wilfred Burtt owned Burtt's Garage in Innage Road for many years until their retirement.) That summer flew by. In the November Leonard and I were engaged and we were married on 28th March 1959 at the Friends' Meeting House, Bournville, surrounded by our families and many friends. We both knew we could not have asked for more love than that shown to us on that happy day.

Shop Life in the 60's

I feel I should write a short account of the way in which a retail grocery shop was run in the early 1960's, if only to enable the reader to make comparison with today's methods.

The day would commence at 8.00 a.m. when Leonard or I would carry sides of bacon and hams from the cold room in the cellar up the stairs to the bacon cupboard situated underneath the provisions counter in the shop. We would then retrace our steps twice more to appear firstly with trays of unsliced cooked meats and finally with the blocks of different types of cheese. This done we would then sort through the order books to see who wanted what, be it a pound of smoked or plain bacon, plain gammon, English cheddar, Caerphilly, Leicester, Gloucester, then slice, cut, weigh and wrap the amount ordered, remembering of course to write the customer's name on the wrapping. Having done this, the packs would be carried to the packing room at the rear of the shop. This whole operation would normally take about 45 minutes which conveniently left 15 minutes in which to unlock the out-buildings, switch on the lights and open up the shop. By 9 o'clock the staff, five female and one male, would have arrived and customers would be at the door as it was unlocked. Most would be young mothers who had seen their offspring safely to school.

The assistants were always busy either serving customers, unpacking goods in the cellar or one of the other storage areas, stacking goods on the shop shelves, making up orders for checking and delivery, or

Some of the staff – 1960.

We offer you
courtesy, service,
everything from
cheapest that is
to the best that m
can buy.

Inside Bournville Village Stores – 1960.

loading the van with goods. They cleaned windows, shelves, floors whenever there was a spillage. A few would work through the normal lunch-time and they would have their break at about 1.30 p.m. After lunch it was all hands to the deck to ensure all the orders were assembled and inevitably there were times when a customer rushed in with an order at the last minute for delivery the same day and a plausible excuse for lateness was always forthcoming.

On Mondays most of the day was taken up with the stacking of shelves which meant endless traipsing up and down stairs backwards and forwards from shop to store to shop carrying heavily laden baskets of tinned goods, cereal packs, soap cartons, bottled goods. Each week, two people were allotted the task of weighing up ½lb. and 1lb. packs of dried fruits, prunes, sultanas, currants and glace cherries – a sticky job if ever there was one – sugar, hazelnuts, almonds, walnuts. Danish butter was still delivered in wooden casks and had to be weighed and packed in the 'Bournville Village Stores' greaseproof paper. Believe me, being a shop assistant in those days was a tiring occupation, legs ached and at times it was difficult to be pleasant when serving a customer. Another job that had to be done at least once a month was the defrosting of the shop refrigerator and no one relished that task; in fact more often than not it was done by Leonard who finished up looking absolutely perished. Nowadays with much more modern appliances I imagine the machines de-frost themselves.

I have already described the vast amount of building that was used as storage space. In those days everything stocked would have been received from wholesalers whose representatives had previously called to gain an order. They would pay a visit at least once a month and goods ordered would be delivered within a few days. I have to admit there were times when such business representatives were not very welcome, but to have the goods delivered was far less wearing than having to go and collect it all from a Cash and Carry, which is the norm today.

As shop closing times approached the bacon and cooked meats slicers had to be dismantled and cleaned thoroughly in hot soapy water, and on more than one occasion a customer would come in for a ½lb. of bacon, which of course meant the cleaning operation had to be gone through all over again. As I write this passage I am reminded of the time when Leonard and I returned home from Meeting for worship one Christmas morning and were greeted by a valued customer who asked if we could cut her some bacon. This was the only time I remember Leonard refusing to serve someone, and to this day I can visualise the look of indignation he received from the customer in question.

Once the shop closed, time was spent generally tidying the premises and then we would retire to the flat above. There always seemed to be plenty of office work to be done in the evenings; filing of customers' bills, checking of delivery order forms, and once a month the typing of accounts, for in those days many folk paid once a month, or, in one or two instances, once a quarter. Each week wages, income tax and national insurance had to be calculated and recorded in huge wages books. Once a year records would be submitted to the Inland Revenue. Cheques had to be written and posted to suppliers. In those days we banked at Lloyds and their cheques at the time were pink. This seemed to have a soporific effect on Leonard as he seemed always to end up falling asleep whenever he had a quantity to write. Maybe the bank in their wisdom changed the colour of their cheques for that reason.

In the middle 60's we purchased a business in a lock-up shop in Swarthmore Road. It had been a branch of Barrow's Stores from the time it was built, and when they relinquished it, we decided we would try to run it alongside our existing business. In fact the premises were very small and didn't cater for a great deal of storage, so whoever purchased it had to be prepared to pay frequent visits to the Cash and Carry or else already have stock from which to draw. With the large premises at Bournville we felt this was practicable and we already were delivering orders to many folk living in the fast-developing area around Swarthmore Road. Things went well for a time, but, with the building of supermarkets and the advent of second car families, shoppers became fickle and before long we were regarded, as many other retailers in our position experienced, as a local convenience where the odd item forgotten at the supermarket could be purchased. The prices we were expected to pay for goods supplied were way above those paid by the big conglomerates; they had the advantage of buying in huge quantities and therefore were offered big discounts. At the same time rents, heating and lighting, petrol and wages were all increasing while custom was declining and the 'little man' suffered greatly as a consequence.

I had envisaged my carrying on the business when Leonard retired, but I could not face the heavy work involved in fetching and carrying heavy goods, coupled together with the anxiety of wondering just how long we would remain solvent, plus running a family home. We therefore sold the business with feelings of regret but with an immense sense of relief for we could see the changes that were taking place with the gradual decline of individual service to the customer. We believed at the time, and I still believe today, that there is a need for small retail outlets to cater for local people, to be there when the individual shopper needs to converse in order to relieve an anxiety or pressure. I feel sure such 'care in the community' would go a long way toward re-establishing a sense of calmness, security and a feeling of being wanted among many folk who these days regard themselves as faceless rejects and just another statistic in the ledger of life.

Another chapter closed.

The Serbian Orthodox Church of St Lazar, Bournville. Built 1965-68.

The Church of St Lazar

The Church is situated at the corner of Cob Lane and Griffins Brook Lane. The building was started in 1965 and was undertaken by both English and Yugoslavian craftsmen, with a hope that it would give political refugees, from the Communist regime in Yugoslavia, a sense that they were not too far removed from their home-land. They had settled in this country after the Second World War and a number were employed by Cadbury Brothers. For many years a room of a large house in Middleton Hall Road, Kings Norton was used as their spiritual home until the completion of the Church of St Lazar in 1968.

The Church is an exact replica of one in Yugoslavia, dedicated to the King St Lazar, and a mosaic to commemorate this fact is found above the main entrance door.

It is of typical Serbian Byzantine design and many of its features originated in Yugoslavia. The marble covering the church's floors comes from the same quarries from which the marble was obtained for the original church. The beautiful hand-beaten copper panels on the

139

main entrance door of the Church, depicting the baptism of Christ, also come from their native country.

The interior decoration is magnificent from the 14th-century wooden screen to the giant metal chandelier symbolising the Divine Crown. Without a doubt the most striking feature of the Church is the huge figure of Christ painted by the Yugoslav artist, Dusan Mihajlovic, which covers the main dome and is surrounded by glorious frescoes.

These show 12 Old Testament Prophets. A truly wonderful memorial to their patron saint and to the skill of the Yugoslav people.

Second Half Century – Schools

The second half century of the life of Bournville has also seen provision made for the education of children living within the ever expanding Estate.

In 1951 Dame Elizabeth Cadbury Secondary Modern School was built in Woodbrooke Road. Over the years, with the fluctuation in the birth rate and changing legislation within the Education system, the School has grown and adapted to meet the requirements of the day. It is now a Secondary School and as I write I am aware of extensions being built to accommodate yet more than the present 640 pupils.

In order to cater for the children of families moving into houses on the Shenley and Lower Shenley Estates, Green Meadow School was built in Green Meadow Road in 1958 and at the time of writing caters for 423 pupils of infant and junior age.

A little earlier, in 1954 and 1955 both Bournville Girls' Technical and Bournville Boys' Technical Schools were opened in Griffins Brook Lane, to cater for those in the senior school age group. By 1970 they were each being referred to as a Grammar/Technical School. In 1973 the two schools were amalgamated and are now called Bournville Secondary School. They have a total of 1,100 pupils on the register.

Northfield Manor Infant and Junior School in Swarthmore Road, adjacent to the Weoley Hill Estate, was built in 1962 and at the present time has 405 children on the register.

In 1978 St Francis of Assisi (C of E) School was opened in Teazel Avenue, Bournville. Catering for 224 children when built it was envisaged it might be extended but the fall in the birth-rate led to this idea being shelved for the time being. It has been pointed out to me that any extension would lead inevitably to the development of the much used Playing Field Area.

In addition to the above mentioned schools St Laurence Church of England School, Bunbury Road, lies just within the boundary of Bournville Estate, and caters for children of infant and junior age.

Shenley Court Comprehensive School, although situated a few hundred yards outside the Estate, is, nevertheless, where a great number of young people of the area move to when reaching senior school age. The registers show 1,500 pupils on the books at the beginning of 1995.

All the schools referred to are recognised as being responsible to the City of Birmingham Education Department.

Our Children

On the 4th April 1959 Leonard and I returned from honeymoon and took up residence in the flat above the Bournville Village Stores. I admit to being a little apprehensive as to how I would be accepted as Mr Broomfield's second wife and furthermore as Peggy's step-mother. In the event I need not have worried, although the first 18 months or so did not go without a certain amount of tension between Peggy and myself, but with perseverance on both our parts and with loving and helpful guidance from Leonard we weathered the storm.

During those first few months Peggy was working at Bournbrook Nursery whilst studying for her NNEB certificate and at the end of the allotted term was successful and as a result managed to secure a permanent job at Steward Street Nursery, where she loved caring for the babies and toddlers. All this was to change due to her meeting a young man at a CND Christmas Party held at Fircroft College in 1960. His name was John Harper, and it was he who encouraged Peggy to further her education by spending a year at Hillcroft College, Surbiton, Surrey. This she did and upon completion of the course she worked for a time in the City of Birmingham Housing Department at Bush House, Broad Street. John in the meantime completed a degree course at Swansea University.

They were married at Birmingham Registry Office on 30th August, 1963, and were to have a succession of homes in Essex, London, South

141

Wales and Sussex. Their first child, a son, Nicholas, was born in February 1966 and they had a second son, Jo, in February 1968.

In 1975 the marriage broke and both Peggy and John encouraged the two boys to stay with their father in Lewes, Sussex, mainly because this would mean their schooling would not be disrupted. This was a very sad and difficult time for Peggy and it was only with the help and support of close friends that she began to come to terms with her position. In 1977 she met and married Mike Lunan, a divorcee, and for a time they were to live in London before moving to Plumpton Green in Sussex, thence back to the Barbican, London, before deciding to start a new life on the Isle of Arran, Scotland in 1988. They still live there and they each have a job which brings them into contact with folk from many walks of life. Peggy's sons and Mike's daughters, although living many miles from Scotland, 'phone home or write fairly frequently. In recent months Peggy has said she regards me as a pal. What more could a step-mother ask?

I had entered marriage hoping that one day Leonard and I would be blessed with a family of our own and in 1961 our son, Jonathan, was born at Loveday Street Maternity Hospital. He was to spend the first eight months of his life at the flat above the shop and then in February 1962 we all moved to a four-bedroom house in Green Meadow Road, Weoley Hill. (As a matter of interest the purchase price was £6,000.) It was from this address that Peggy was married. When she left home we kept the large house for some years, always hoping for a second child, and realising that if one of my parents died we would have sufficient room to accommodate the survivor if need be. In the event my mother was diagnosed as terminally ill in March 1969 and she died in September that year. Her death was a shattering blow to us all, especially my father. He never really regained his strength and in February 1970 he too was diagnosed as being terminally ill. He died in June 1970, just three weeks before Leonard and I had a daughter, Rachel.

By this time it had become blatantly obvious that with the advent of mini-markets and the promise of supermarkets the future for the local grocery retailer was bleak indeed. Sufficient to say we decided to find a smaller home. We moved to 27 Fox Hill, Weoley Hill, in August 1970 when Rachel was just six weeks old and later that month my sister was married thus creating another piece of family history.

Leonard retired in 1973 and for a while he worked part-time for the Margery Fry Trust at their offices in Selly Oak. A few months later he suffered a stroke which left him immobile for a time; what was more

Marian and Edgar Owen.

disturbing was that it deprived him of his speech and although some improvement was made in that quarter his vocabulary was to remain considerably curtailed. He, as you can imagine, was very frustrated.

Shortly afterwards we heard of a bungalow in Green Meadow Road being for sale and we successfully negotiated with the vendors and moved yet again in February 1975. The next few years were difficult for Leonard, but in spite of failing health he rarely complained. He took each day as it came and did what he could to help in the house and garden as and when he was able. He found a new hobby and spent many hours repairing clocks for friends and neighbours. Gradually he became less well and in December 1978 he passed away peacefully.

By this time Jonathan, who had been a pupil at Northfield Manor School before moving on to Shenley Court Comprehensive School, was working for a retail television company in Kings Heath and Rachel was attending Northfield Manor School. She too was to go on to Shenley Court School in due course.

In 1983 Jonathan met Denise Wood of Kings Heath and they were married the following year. Sadly they have now separated and are going through divorce proceedings. Their son, Jonathan junior, is living with his father and is at present a pupil at one of the local junior schools. He hopes to move to a Bournville secondary school in September 1995.

Upon leaving Shenley Court School Rachel went on to higher education and studied at Westhill/Newman Colleges before graduating from Birmingham University in July 1993. She now teaches at Raddlebarn School in Selly Oak.

Since my husband's death I have worked variously as Deputy Warden at Oak Tree House, Bournville and as a cleaner for individual elderly or needy people within my home area. I am fortunate that although I retired a few years ago, many of the folk I worked for still keep in touch.

The Estate in the 80's

By 1984 the Bournville Estate covered an area of 1,000 acres and there were 7,500 dwellings. By this time land available for development was at a premium.

In 1988 33 houses and bungalows, including 14 for rent to the elderly, were built on Woodbrooke Meadow, referred to by many of my generation and others as 'Roy's Field', for it was there the horses from Roy's, the bakers on the Green, retired to each night after a hard day's work. The undertaking was the responsibility of Bournville Village Developments Limited, a wholly owned subsidiary of the Bournville Village Trust Group.

I was not alone when I objected to the plans for the development of the area and I still mourn the passing of the meadow with all the beauty it offered at the different seasons of the year. To me it was a wonderful back-drop to the yachting pool and I have witnessed many folk throughout the years just sitting in a car, may be recovering from a spell in hospital or perhaps just frail and infirm in their later years, quietly admiring the scene and the feeling of peace it invoked.

Mrs Rita Wallace of Oak Tree Lane was another objector and wrote expressing firm opposition to the Scheme. The following was written by her and printed in *The Carillon* Bournville Village News. She has kindly agreed for me to quote her article in full.

> I was born in Oak Tree Lane, Bournville. My parents had married at Harborne Church and settled in Bournville.

The Gateway – Griffins Brook House 1915. Now C. L. Holding & Sons, Builders, Charfield Close.

We were on the edge of Bournville Estate overlooking miles of fields and countryside. Cadbury Brothers had built the Estate, but our house and the one adjoining were owned by a private land-lord, who had previously lived in one of them. We were virtually in the country; it was a walk of 20 minutes to Selly Oak or Stirchley for shops and trams which ran into Birmingham from both these villages.

Opposite us was Yew Tree Farm where I remember going to get milk, cream, etc. The dairy was down three steps very cold and the milk was in churns with different measures hanging round the edge, all made of copper. Later it ceased to be a farm, and became stabling for Roy's (the bakers) horses.

Just up the road was the cinder path, a footpath cutting through the fields to the Bristol Road, used later as a way to the trams when the track was extended to the Lickey and Rubery. We children played in the fields always full of long meadow grass and of course the brook which ran through them. A large muddy pond was surrounded by bulrushes and full of newts and frogs. We invariably fell in, much to our parents' annoyance.

At the end of the path was Lucas Farm where they kept a dairy herd. Behind was a large house surrounded by trees. The house (Griffins Brook House) has long gone and the land is now used as a car park, but the gateway remains and is the entrance to C. L. Holding and Sons premises in Cob Lane. We children said the place was haunted and always ran past.

145

Rear view – Yew Tree Farm, Oak Tree Lane.

But sentiment does not count for much these days, and people need homes; objections were over-ruled and development of Wood-brooke Meadow went ahead. At the time it was reported that interest for all the properties was high, particularly for the rented bungalows with some 400 people applying for one.

The properties for sale ranged in price from £115,000 to £210,000. The scheme was opened by Sir Adrian Cadbury on 19th June 1990. The revenue from the sale of the private houses was to finance the building of the rented properties.

Each unit is orientated to the sun with triple-glazed windows and fully insulated 11mm cavity walls. No tropical hardwoods have been used, the only hardwood utilised being Canadian western red cedar.

Landscaping has been provided at a cost of £2,000 per unit.

146

Queen Mother Court (opened 1970).

Selly Wood House (built 1980).

Each individual home has burglar alarms, smoke detectors, cable TV (12 channels) and fully fitted kitchen.

The bungalows for the elderly have a 24-hour warden link.

Part of the area is named 'Harvey Mews', after Bournville's first architect, W. Alexander Harvey.

Bonner House (built 1970).

Pocklington Place (built 1975).

148

Christopher Taylor Court, Rowheath (built 1986).

Rosefields (built early 1980's).

Laurence Court (built 1983).

Housing Specialised

During the past 35 years much has been done to alleviate the problems of those in need of specialised accommodation, be they elderly, single parents, young children, people with impaired vision.

One of the first such projects was OAK TREE HOUSE. Opened on 28th November 1964 by Kenneth and Phyllis Southall it stands next to the Bournville Village Trust Offices in Oak Tree Lane.

The building, originally built to provide accommodation for retired members of the Society of Friends, with a proviso that others should be considered in the event of no Friend requiring accommodation when a flat becomes vacant, is made up of 17 flats or bed-sits for single people, two flats for married couples and the Warden's living quarters, together with a communal dining-room and a spacious sitting-room.

Residents provide their own furnishings. A mid-day meal, cooked in the well-equipped kitchen, is provided each day of the year, and residents cater for other meals themselves. There are two guest-rooms, the usual utility rooms, providing laundering facilities and drying area, and garages are available for those with cars. It is built on land leased from

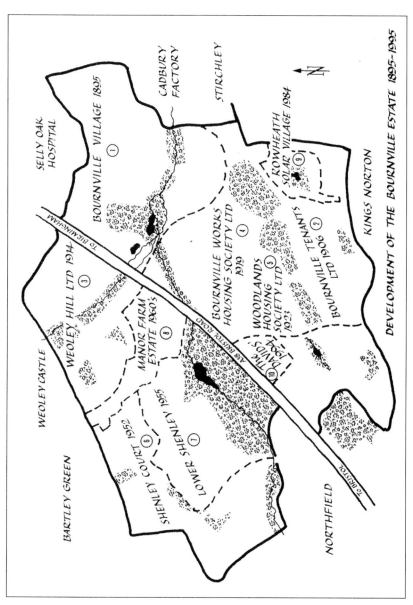

Development of the Bournville Estate 1895-1995.

Selly Wood – demolished to make way for Queen Mother Court.

Bournville Village Trust and stands in a well tended garden area. It is managed by a committee, appointed by Warwickshire Monthly Meeting of the Society of Friends, the members of which have responsibility for the general upkeep of the fabric of the place and the well-being of the residents. It is continually being brought up to date in numerous ways to bring it in to line with health and safety regulations of the day.

The development of an area of land immediately to the south of the Woodlands Royal Orthopaedic Hospital during the 70's and 80's resulted in 243 dwellings, consisting of flats and houses being built for rent. At about the same time, flats to accommodate 99 single people were built in Griffins Brook lane.

Work was also going ahead with the construction of flats for retired members of the teaching profession. Although built on similar lines to those of Oak Tree House, the construction itself is larger and consequently caters for a greater number of residents. Otherwise the facilities offered are similar. The cost was met by funds from the Teachers' Benevolent Fund. The premises, situated in Selly Wood Road, were opened by Queen Elizabeth the Queen Mother on 6th May 1970 and carry the name QUEEN MOTHER COURT.

By August 1980 SELLY WOOD HOUSE, standing next to Queen Mother Court, was nearing completion and applications for accommodation from elderly infirm were being considered. At that time, those requiring long term nursing or hospital treatment were not accepted. However, in recent years, the Home applied for and was granted dual registration which has meant such people are now taken as residents. The project, built by The Teachers' Benevolent Fund and furbished by that body together with Bournville Village Trust and The Society of Friends, provides furnished single bed-sitting rooms, together with all meals and nursing care. The scheme is run by a Manager and several Care Assistants, with support from domestic staff. It is administered by a Management Committee comprised of four representatives of each of the three bodies mentioned.

A service such as this is very necessary and costly. However those applying, whether they be a Bournville resident, a retired teacher or a member of the Society of Friends should not be intimidated by the initial charges as some assistance might be available through Social Services, depending of course on each individual applicant's financial circumstances.

Built in 1986, CHRISTOPHER TAYLOR COURT is a sheltered housing scheme for elderly people, consisting of 42 flats, plus a Warden's house, common room and a small laundry. Six of the flats have been designed to accommodate wheel-chair users. All are accessible without using stairways. The Warden and staff provide 24-hour cover. The building is heated to 16 degrees centigrade and the flats themselves to 21 degrees centigrade. It is laid out around two open-ended courtyards, on land that slopes down to the north, but which catches a great deal of sun to the south. The majority of the flats are in the south-facing wings with corridors, facing the courtyard, running along the north side. A central block running north-south contains the common-room, sitting area, laundry and boiler-room. The whole building is a part of the Rowheath Solar Village, which comprises nearly 300 dwellings on seven separate sites.

In 1982 the Bournville Village Trust negotiated with Cadbury Schweppes and the City of Birmingham for the purchase of 65 acres of land at Rowheath and this is where the ROWHEATH SOLAR VILLAGE began in 1984. It was planned with energy conservation of paramount importance. All dwellings are orientated to maximum solar gain aiming to achieve unshaded, south-facing windows from 9 a.m. to 3 p.m. each day of the year. The buildings are constructed with ground floor concrete partition walls, a concrete ground floor, and 100mm concrete inner leaf to all external walls. All windows are double-glazed. Heat reflector roller-blinds are fitted to all windows for use during the hours of darkness. Detailed monitoring of the village was carried out, with sensors being read every few minutes round the clock, by computers. A completely automated weather station also provided further data which assisted in understanding what was happening at each property and the advantages and disadvantages of all the particular features. The project was, at the time, the largest Solar Village in Western Europe and was supported by the Commission for the European Communities.

THE PARKLANDS development was completed in 1985 and the demonstration house attracted international interest at an Open Day in September that year. Twenty-three houses and bungalows in the scheme were for sale on the open market. In addition, bungalows designed by Bournville Village Trust Architects for the Waterloo Housing Association under the Government's Leasehold Scheme for the Elderly were also completed.

ROWHEATH HOUSE, built earlier, but nevertheless a part of the foregoing area, has accommodation for 42 residents and each flat has a pull cord connecting it to a Warden call-system. Cover is provided by the Warden, deputy and staff for eight hours each day. The system is linked to a central control unit in Christopher Taylor Court which means that when the Warden of Rowheath House is not on duty calls are relayed and dealt with by the Warden there.

LAURENCE COURT, was built by the St Laurence Bournville Village Trust Housing Association in 1983 on approximately 1.2 acres and provides 22 retirement flats. It is situated on land that had originally been the site of a Priory belonging to an Order of Nuns, The Sisters of Charity. The front gardens contain several magnificent mature trees including Cedar, Oak and Sweet Chestnut. The buildings are based around a central court with all the entrances facing inwards. Eighteen flats have two bedrooms and the remainder have one. Each

154

Woodbrooke Meadow Development with Valley Parkway in the foreground.

flat is fully fitted with gas-fired central heating and for the convenience of residents and the gas and electric services, meters are housed inside a shared bin-store. These, together with the fitting of entry phones to all upstairs flats provide a safeguard for the residents from the security angle. There is a pull-cord system (in bathroom and main bedroom) in each flat which rings out in the Priory, and also lights up an indicator lamp outside the front door of the flat concerned. If need be the stairways can be adapted to take chair-lifts.

The flats were sold through a local agent at prices ranging from £20,000 to £24,000. The subsidy from the Housing Corporation was 30% and the above prices represent the remaining 70%. Six lock-up garages were included in the scheme and were sold for £1,000 each.

The service charges in 1987 for a one-bedroomed flat was £33.00 per month, and a two-bedroomed flat £35.00 per month. This covered the maintenance of the building, external painting, insurance, maintenance of the grounds, the emergency alarm system, external lighting and the communal television system. Any re-sale has to be made through the Association at the impartial opinion of value by an independent Valuer. Lessees have to pay the legal costs of both the

Association and their own solicitor when buying, and they may not purchase their freehold. Bournville Village Trust had had close links with the Sisters of Charity for some time, having been consultant architects when their Priory was re-built in 1978 following the purchase of a plot of surplus land from them in order to build a residential warden-controlled sheltered scheme, ROSEFIELDS, to which the Sisters act as Wardens.

Other buildings on Bournville that have been built to house those with special needs are BONNER HOUSE, built in 1970 and situated in Selly Wood Road, a block of self-contained flats for unmarried mothers administered by the National Childrens Homes. There are 10 flats and the residents cater for themselves.

POCKLINGTON PLACE, a residential home for the blind, situated in Hole Lane and built through the generous gift of Thomas Pocklington. PROSPECT HALL, built in 1975 on land belonging to SELLY OAK COLLEGES, caters for physically disabled people and was opened by Queen Elizabeth the Queen Mother in 1977. At present it is run by Birmingham Social Services Department.

In 1985 two houses were built on the site of the original Slater's Haulage Contractors yard (later Hanwell's Dairy and more recently Birmingham Dairies depot), in Selly Oak Road. They were designed specifically to accommodate families who include a physically handicapped member of their number. The accommodation allows for the disabled person to occupy an area of the house, having all the necessary facilities on one level whilst enjoying a normal life with the rest of the family.

Four houses in Raddlebarn Road were converted in 1989 in order to provide accommodation for five residents with learning difficulties.

As we enter 1995, work has begun on a conversion project at a former garage in Raddlebarn Road. It is envisaged the existing property will eventually offer a Group Home, for people with a learning disability, together with two flats and a house. These three residential units will then be let to appropriate people from the Trust's waiting lists. At the same time flats are to be built on a small site in Jervoise Drive.

The above indicates the amount of research and development that has been carried out and is continuing to be done by Bournville Village Trust in order to provide various types of housing for those with special needs.

Leasehold Reform Act 1967

I think it is true to say that there has been very little in the way of conflict between Bournville Village Trustees and residents during the life-time of Bournville. However, one recent case was an exception and came about as the indirect result of the Leasehold Reform Act of 1967.

The passing of the 1967 Leasehold Reform Act enabled leasholders to purchase the freehold of their properties after a qualifying period of residence. In order to protect the amenity of the Estate, and so that the Trust could retain a measure of control over future developments, a Scheme of Management was obtained from the High Court in 1972.

Briefly THE BOURNVILLE VILLAGE TRUST SCHEME includes the following:

> The object of the Scheme is to ensure for the benefit of tenants of houses buildings and land in the Scheme Area that the standards of appearance and amenity (whether existing or future) in the Scheme Area shall be preserved and not deteriorate by reason of any tenant of a house in the Scheme Area acquiring the freehold of the house either under the enfranchisement provision of the Act or under an arrangement entered into apart from such Act.

> A tenant who has acquired the freehold of any property in the Scheme Area . . . shall be under an obligation to and be deemed to have covenanted with the landlord for the time being properly to maintain and keep in good repair the exterior of and the internal structural parts of such building to the satisfaction of the landlord for the time being in all respects.

> The freeholder of any home in the Scheme Area . . . shall make payments to the landlord;

> a) On demand, any sum previously expended by the landlord in the maintenance and repair of such house or for carrying out work to remedy any failure in respect of such house to comply with the scheme.

> b) On demand shall pay to the landlord a due proportion as certified by the landlord's Surveyor of any sum previously expended by the landlord in the maintenance and repair of any property.

c) On demand shall pay to the landlord in respect of such house on the 31st December in any year in respect of the year ending on such date the sum of £3 towards the provision supervision or maintenance by the landlord . . . of services facilities or amenities in the Scheme Area provided that at or after the end of every fifth year of the Scheme and in respect of the five years next following such fifth year the payment due in respect of any such years may at the discretion of the landlord be increased Provided that any such increased payment shall not exceed a sum arrived at by multiplying the said sum of £3 by a fraction whereof the numerator shall be the General Retail Prices Index issued by the authority of Her Majesty's Government and applicable on the 31st December of the appropriate fifth year and the denominator shall be the General Retail Prices Index applicable on the 31st December 1969.

In October 1987 residents received correspondence from Bournville Village Trust notifying them that the Estate Management Scheme Committee had approved an increase in the management charge from £13.22 to £16.82 plus Value Added Tax to take effect from 1st January 1987. The letter also went on to say that since the Scheme of Management was introduced the cost of maintaining the facilities on the Estate had risen much faster than the increase in the contribution made by freeholders and leaseholders towards those costs. The Trustees, therefore, resolved to apply to the High Court for a variation of the Scheme to bring the management charge into line with costs. Residents were told they would be given the opportunity to comment on the proposal before it was formally presented to the Scheme Committee and the Trustees for final approval.

In April 1989 freeholders and leaseholders again received correspondence from the Trust informing them that since the correspondence of 23rd October 1987, public meetings had been held at which the Trustees' proposal had been considered. As a result of a number of points relating to the proposed application to the Court had emerged including a suggestion, which was adopted, that there should be a provision that if 10% of the freeholders lodged objections, the amount of the expenditure on which the charge was based would be liable to be revised by an independent surveyor. The Trustees agreed to this suggestion which was accordingly incorporated in the proposed wording to be submitted to the Court. Residents were asked to consider whether they wished to oppose the application and, if so, to be joined as a defendant to these Court proceedings.

Upon reading the above information I replied pointing out that being a life-long resident of Bournville and a Quaker of many years standing, I considered careful dialogue between two parties, as and when differences of opinion occur, should in turn lead to genuine reconciliation. I opposed the Trust's application but did not wish to be tied to action in a Court of Law. I felt it necessary for freeholders and leaseholders to be given more opportunity to meet with representatives of the Trustees so that they could submit a full case report.

I was not alone in my objection to the Trust's proposals; others claimed they would mean freeholders would face an open-ended charge and this could mean a 50% increase – possibly every year. Questions were asked as to what had happened to the capital sums raised as the result of payment for freeholds; we had been led to believe they would be invested to produce the equivalent of the lease-hold ground rent.

In April 1989, members of the Society of Friends resident in the Bournville Village Trust Area wrote to the Trust's Registrar, expressing their concern about the situation of confrontation that had developed between residents and the Trust, and they asked the Bournville Village Trust to seek a stay of hearing to the Court for the purpose of creating an opportunity for further consultation between the residents and members of the Scheme of Management.

On the 8th June 1989 Bournville Freeholders' and Leaseholders' Action Consortium was set up. Its members were freeholders and leaseholders in Bournville who were concerned about the Trust's proposals and the increase in charges predicted. Its objects were to negotiate with the Trust and if necessary to go to court to contest the Trust's application.

Representatives of the Freeholders' and Leaseholders' Action Consortium and of the Society of Friends and other interested parties met informally with the Trustees in mid June in order to substantiate the claims made. Those who attended were grateful for having had the opportunity to meet with Trustees to raise matters that were of concern to many residents, but ultimately we accepted that the case would have to be heard in court.

On October 11th 1991, Mr Ian McTear, the Environment Correspondent of *The Birmingham Post* wrote under the heading,

COURT MAY END THE BATTLE OF BOURNVILLE

A long-running battle over who pays to keep tidy one of Birmingham's most famous model communities is about to go to court. The case will decide whether the wealthier residents in Bournville Village pay more for keeping it clean. It started more than two years ago, when Bournville Village Trust decided its 1,300 freeholders were not paying a fair share of the management fee. The fee is spent on the upkeep of the 1,000-acre Estate. By law the fee is reviewed every five years and adjusted in line with the retail price index. Last year the bill amounted to £200,000 of which £21,000 was paid by freeholders.

Mr McTear went on to report that Bournville Trust wanted to double the annual freehold fee to £40, but that that could not be done without High Court approval. The Trust had applied to make the change two years previously, and a ruling would be made at the High Court in Birmingham after a five-day hearing, due to start on November 26th.

In November 1991, *The Birmingham Post* carried a report of the Court's decision headed,

HOMEOWNERS ORDERED TO PAY OUT A TIDY SUM

The reporter, Mr Ian McTear wrote;

Homeowners in one of Birmingham's most famous model communities have lost their long-running battle over who pays to keep it tidy. . . .

Yesterday Judge Nathaniel Micklem ruled in favour of the Trust, clearing the way for it to raise the freeholders' contribution. . . . Judge Micklem said Trustees were free to set the charge at any level, as long as they acted in an economic and efficient manner. The freeholders are not paying their appropriate share. . . . Dr John Woodward who acted as representative defendant said, 'We are very disappointed. The Trust has got the extra power it wanted. If the freeholders are to recover some of their position they will have to scrutinise the way the Trust carries out the maintenance tasks, seeing that they are necessary and carried out efficiently and economically.'

Mr James Wilson, the Trust's chief executive said; 'This is a good decision for the community in Bournville. It enables the Trustees to provide high-quality housing in what is an attractive environment.'

Writing some three years after the High Court Hearing, with the privilege of hindsight, I feel those who objected to the initial proposals were right in their deliberations because there were those who were expressing concern with regard to the deterioration of the maintenance of the Estate. Hedges had been left to become overgrown and unsightly, pathways in the parks were being neglected, grass cutting had been minimised. Even with the present-day policies of environmental management and conservation, no one wanted the neighbourhood to become an eyesore. The question on every Freeholder's lips was 'Why am I paying so much more in charges and seeing a deterioration in the standard of maintenance?' Everyone is aware of the wishes of the Founder, to provide housing for those in need, but I do not believe he would have approved of money being spent in other areas whilst his beloved Bournville was beginning to look neglected.

Having lived on Bournville land all my life I am able to remember the days when trees, footpaths, grass verges were all kept tidy and in good order by workers employed by the Trust; people who took a pride in the work they did. Over the years, less and less has been done by Bournville Trust employees; maintenance has been handed over to Birmingham City Council and others who presumably work to Trustees' wishes.

A matter which greatly worries residents is the way in which some newcomers to the area seem not to be aware of the fact that the neighbourhood is the delightful place it is, due in no small measure to the careful planning and diligence of those who have gone before. The Trustees have always made known the need for residents to be thoughtful when considering alteration or extensions to their property, and have urged them to keep within the limits set out in their publication *Design Guidelines for Altering or Improving Your Home*. Visitors on a tour of the Estate might well wonder how the plans for some extensions have been passed, 'tho tastefully designed and better built alterations do outnumber the not so good.

I can accept that it is nigh on impossible for prospective buyers of a property within the area to have knowledge of the wishes of the Trustees unless the vendor is prepared to make the facts known when selling his property. It seems to me it might be politic to remind anyone showing an interest in becoming a resident that the area is covered by a Scheme of Management. To quote from *Design Guidelines*;

> We, that is the Trust and yourselves can now only preserve and enhance the special environment throughout the Estate by ensuring that any new development or alteration work is considered within the context of the architectural style of your own and your neighbour's property and the surrounding area.

Who would disagree?

There were those who were disappointed when the High Court ruled in favour of the Trust; nevertheless differences of opinion had been expressed and doubtful matters, in most cases, clarified. The whole costly exercise, whilst regrettable at the time, must surely have led to the healing of a rift that had opened up between the Trust, freeholders, leasholders, and tenants, a fact I find encouraging as the Village celebrates its centenary.

The Final Decade

In 1991 six new bungalows for sale to the elderly were completed in Summerfield Drive off Shenley Gardens, on the site of the Hawkestone Road Tennis Court.

Now in 1995 work is going well with the development of 15 acres of land at 'The Davids' in Hole Lane, formerly the home of Laurence and Joyce Cadbury and their family. The site was sold to Wimpey Homes, in a £4m deal in 1993 and building is being carried out by them and Berkeley Homes (Midlands) Limited. Wimpey Homes are to build 36 four-bedroom homes, while Berkeley Homes will be constructing 12 five-bedroom and 19 four-bedroom houses in their standard design. All the properties are to be detached, with garages, landscaped surroundings and with good vehicle and pedestrian access. I understand the plans drawn up by Wimpey and Berkeley were submitted to Bournville Village Trust for approval. This could well be the final large development to take place on the Bournville Estate, as available land is almost non-existent.

The last decade has seen the closure of two retail outlets on Bournville Village Green, one being replaced by Bigwood BVT Ltd, an estate agency, and the other by a new Bournville Village Trust Area

Building in progress at 'The Davids'.

Office. This means residents can now arrange to purchase a property, use the facilities of a bank, post office, electricians/gift shop, ladies outfitters, butchers, hairdressers, toys/gift shop, chemist and news-agent, together with a doctor's surgery, but are unable to purchase a week's groceries or fresh vegetables, a sure indication that super-markets have had a big influence on today's marketing of those partic-ular products.

During the last 35 years there have been many changes in the way in which both the retailer and the customer have gone about their busi-ness. No longer are goods delivered to the retailer from the manufac-turer. Privately run grocery or greengrocery businesses can ill afford the privilege of free delivery to their customers nowadays. Recently a local daily newspaper carried a headline 'Shop locally if you want to save town, buyers told.' Could the same be said of the shops in Bournville, I wonder? I fear the answer might be yes.

The last 30 years have, as a result of automation and the introduc-tion of continental shifts, seen a vast reduction in the number of people employed by Cadbury Schweppes. Bournville Trust itself no longer employs anything like the number of painters, carpenters, plumbers, bricklayers and like tradesmen as in the days before the war. As in all villages, towns, cities, lifestyles in Bournville have changed dramatically in the last century. People have to move about from one place to another to find work. No longer can one expect to stay in one area throughout one's life-time.

So what of the future?

Professor Gordon Cherry, Chairman of Bournville Village Trust, in his New Year message 1995 writes thus:

> As you will be aware by now, 1995 is an important year for the Trust. It is right we should be marking the centenary throughout the year in many ways. 1995 is neither the end of an era nor the beginning of something new; rather it is a stepping stone, in a long process of growth, change and adaptation. Our environment does not remain static as though preserved in aspic, neither does our community necessarily keep its former features; both environment and community inevitably change over time. So it is with Bournville.

Professor Cherry goes on to remind us that the Trust's current aims are those going back to the earliest days of the Estate.

a) To promote new social housing of good quality.

b) To manage housing and estates to best standards.

c) To encourage residents to share in the decisions affecting them.

He continues:

> George Cadbury's Deed of Foundation was concerned with more than the building of a single model village. His concerns were with meeting the needs of the population 'in and around Birmingham and elsewhere in Great Britain'.

Professor Cherry tells us:

> In 1995 we shall see a Trust, not content to bask in a hundred years of history, but determined to be on the move, as the Founder directed.
>
> In Bordesley, Birmingham, Bournville Village Trust will develop the Village Centre with flats, shops and a dentist's surgery.

164

It is hoped houses for rent will be built in Bartley Green, Birmingham.

Houses in Telford and elsewhere in Shropshire will come on stream.

One or two schemes in Redditch, Hereford and Worcestershire, will be started.

Returning to Bournville, a range of housing and community initiatives will be implemented and traffic calming schemes will be carried out in the Village.

On the Trust's agricultural estates, farm and housing improvement schemes will roll forward.

The Trust Group will continue to offer property care and architectural consultancy.

In recent years, much money has been poured into a variety of projects nationwide, aimed solely at uncovering the way in which our ancestors lived, worked and played but a few generations ago. As a result we now have, within easy travelling distance of Bournville, several centres, such as the Ironbridge Gorge Museum, Black Country Museum, Severn Valley Railway, to say nothing of the rejuvenation of the canal system in and around Birmingham, and the opening up of Cadbury World in August 1990.

Could it be that one day the Bournville Estate will be regarded as a place of historical interest, if in fact that day has not already arrived?

Appendices

Weoley Hill

1914 saw the commencement of building work in the Weoley Hill area. All work was undertaken by Weoley Hill Limited, a Public Utility Society registered in 1913 and funded by Bournville Village Trust. Although the country was at war, building continued until 1917 by which time the houses on the Bristol Road, immediately opposite the entrance to Woodbrooke, and others in Witherford Way, from Bristol Road to the planned junction with Fox Hill, were completed. The houses were built in blocks of two, four or six, and all offered three-bedroom accommodation. Prices ranged from £235 to £290 and there was a 2½% discount for cash. Ground rent was about 2d. per square yard. Because of various restrictions brought about by the war, building was halted in 1917. Re-started in 1919, work began with the construction of dwellings in the area we now know as the uppermost part of Weoley Hill and Fox Hill.

From records, it would appear that some properties suffered damage during the 1914-18 war, due to the firing of an anti-aircraft gun which was situated at the corner of Fox Hill and Weoley Hill. Damage, however, did not amount to much more than a few broken slates. It is said the gun was fired against Zeppelins raiding the Austin munitions factory at Longbridge.

In 1916 the Gardeners' Association was formed and proved to be of great help to new residents. As with Bournville Village Gardeners' Association arrangements were made so that residents could hire tools, and free advice was readily available from those versed in the subject of horticulture. Lectures were arranged and a prize scheme for the best garden was born, together with the organisation of the mounting of an Annual Flower Show. The latter soon became the highlight of the Village year, and for several years prior to the Second World War my father would mount a garden landscaping display.

Following the end of the First World War the continuation of building was undertaken by contractors, but before long, Weoley Hill Limited formed a direct labour department and it was responsible, with one or two exceptions, for the building of all houses on the Estate until the outbreak of World War Two in September 1939. The Estate had its own little estate office, situated at the western end of Weoley Hill, and it remained there until the present bungalows and garages were built in Weoley Hill and on the approach to the cricket field.

Weoley Hill Village Hall was built in 1925 and the Village Council has met there regularly ever since. The Hall proved to be a great asset to village life for many years and was used by many different groups as a venue for socialising, and it is only in recent years that it has become a burden to local residents and the Trust due in no small measure to the perpetrators of vandalism and the consequent increases in maintenance and running costs.

In the mid-30's, a large Home was built at the corner of Middle Park Road and Swarthmore Road for the City of Birmingham District Nursing Association (Selly Oak, Kings Norton and Northfield Area). *The Bournville Village Council Year Book* for 1938 tells us:

> The nurses visit a patient once or twice daily as required, provided a doctor is in attendance. The destitute poor, old-age pensioners and contributors to the Hospitals Contributory Scheme are nursed free. For others a small charge is made. During 1936 the seven nurses in the area paid 30,163 visits.

In recent times the house has been used as a hostel for homeless people and those with learning difficulties.

The plans for Weoley Hill Estate anticipated 650 dwellings and by 1939, 493 houses were complete. The customary roads, sewers and gas and electric services were provided and provision was made for ample open spaces such as the valley parkway, a continuation of the green corridor from Bournville Park through the Valley Park (yachting pool) to Weoley Hill as far as Shenley Fields Road, which is the boundary line. As was the case with previous developments in the area, existing forest trees were preserved whenever practicable, as can be seen in the central reservation of Weoley Hill, and a great many new trees were planted to form the spinneys in Hemyock and Bryony Roads.

My uncle and aunt, Albert and Jessie Guest, were the first owners of 59 Middle Park Road. They moved there in 1930 and my cousin Brian was born there in 1931.

From photographs of the 20's it is evident that the local tennis courts were where the present day bowling green is. Previous to that the first tennis courts were in Fox Hill, on the land that now lies between the two rows of bungalows in Fox Hill Close.

The Bowling Club began its days on the lawns of George Cadbury Jnr's home, Primrose Hill, Bristol Road. However, in 1928 the crown green in the parkway was ready for use and a steady stream of bowlers have used the facility ever since.

The following year, a square of 'hallowed turf' was laid in the parkway between Weoley Hill and Shenley Fields Road, and cricket has been played there more or less continually from that time. The Cricket Club took over the disused Scouts' hut and used it as a pavilion.

The outbreak of the Second World War in 1939 led to a steady reduction in the social life of Weoley Hill, as in other areas. Some organisations managed to keep going. The cricket club still fielded a team, but had to arrange 'play away' matches, as the cricket field, apart from the hallowed square, was under cultivation for 'Dig for Victory'. The Village Hall became the responsibility of the Bournville Village Trust for the duration and the centre was used as an ARP post.

The locality suffered its share of air-raid damage with nos. 41 and 43 Fox Hill and 51 Witherford Way being destroyed, and houses on the north west side of Weoley Hill were badly shaken by a large bomb which landed in a local back garden. The demolished houses mentioned were replaced and the area is now the site of a two-storey block of flats and a small detached bungalow.

As in the rest of the country, street parties were arranged for fire-watching and fighting fires and for mutual aid in general.

When peace arrived and with its continued clothes rationing and general austerity, things did begin to get back to normal if only gradually. In 1946 building re-commenced with Bournville Village Trust direct labour department working in Erica Close, and Bryant's, building under contract to BVT, continuing the row of houses in Shenley Fields Road from Erica Close toward Longbow Road. With the development of land at Lower and Upper Shenley Farms and Yew Tree Farm the green corridor between Weoley Hill and Northfield disappeared.

In the 60's the open ground to the east of Weoley Hill adjacent to Swarthmore Road, the Manor Grounds and the Bristol Road was utilised with the construction of Middle Park Farm Estate consisting of high and low rise blocks of flats, and a group of shops. The flats are now owned by the City and administered by its Housing Department. The Weoley Hill Village Council gave a great deal of help with the setting up of Middle Park Farm Residents' Association and that body still liaises with Weoley Hill Council.

It was around this time that the present day Birmingham College of Further Education on Bristol Road was built.

Weoley Hill Estate Office, 1966.

The final phase of housing on the Weoley Hill Estate was completed in the early 1960's with the building of bungalows in Tamarisk Close and houses in Mimosa Close together with the extending of Bryony Road and Green Meadow Road to meet up with the newly developing Shenley Estate. Other developments took place in the area in the 60's and 70's with the building of a small group of shops and bungalows in Swarthmore Road and houses and flats in Hornbeam Close. They were built under a co-ownership scheme.

Tillyard Croft, a cul-de-sac off Shenley Fields Road, was developed by Birmingham COPEC Housing Improvement Society. (This Society had been formed following a conference of Christian Churches – the Conference on Christian Politics, Economics and Citizenship – in 1924.) Flats and bungalows were built and let to elderly, and more recently to handicapped and unemployed, citizens. Land on one side of the Croft was retained by Bournville Village Trust and houses were built to individual purchasers' requirements.

Opened in 1955, Bryony House, also built by COPEC, provided accommodation for elderly infirm people who found themselves in need of light nursing. It was designed to cater for 35 residents in rooms

171

for one or two people. Over the years it has been modernised and extended and at the present time 40 people are catered for. As I write I learn that plans are under way for refurbishment to take place in the near future.

Weoley Hill Church

Mention must be made of the most prominent building on Weoley Hill and I am indebted to Margaret Glen of Selly Oak and John Bartlett of Bourne Heath, for allowing me to use the following extracts from their book *An Account of Weoley Hill United Reformed Church 1915-1983*.

> The first Church building on Weoley Hill Estate was a YMCA hut that had been removed from Stafford and re-erected on a temporary site in Witherford Way (where houses numbers 56 and 58 now stand). This was rented to the congregation, referred to as Weoley Hill Church, by Weoley Hill Limited at a rent of ½d. per square yard for seven years. It was a Union congregation having members of other denominations as Associate Members and many students of the Selly Oak Colleges attending services, as well as local residents, and was accepted by the Bournville Village Trust as the only church to be built in the suburb of Weoley Hill.

> Early plans show a site for a church in a village centre at the junction of Weoley Hill and Witherford Way, and, a little later, a site on the west side of Fox Hill south of Witherford Way for a permanent building when funds permitted.

> A Presbytery Visitation in 1927 recorded that the congregation had 32 members, 26 associate members and there was a Sunday School of 43 children and 5 teachers.

> In November 1929 an appeal for the building fund for £4,500 was launched and by March 1930 £3,182 had been given or promised.

> In place of the proposed site in Fox Hill the Bournville Village Trust gave freehold the present much more favourable site at the junction of Green Meadow and Bryony Roads. The foundation stone was laid on the 11th January 1933 by Mrs George Cadbury and on 1st July that year the church was dedicated at an opening service.

The building was designed to accommodate 350 people, and in addition to the church it had two large and two small classrooms, vestry, kitchen and cloakrooms.

Since those early days, Weoley Hill Church, in common with other buildings of the same era, has been extended and refurbished, and now not only caters for Sunday Services but also is the venue for Youth Club, Scouts, Guides, and other community groups.

Bournville Almshouses

Bournville Almshouses can be found at the northern end of Bournville. They occupy land at the corner of Linden Road and Maryvale Road. Strictly speaking they are not a part of Bournville Village as such, having been built by George Cadbury's brother, Richard Cadbury. Begun in 1898 they were built to the design of the architect Ewen Harper. Originally 33 in number, each bungalow provided accommodation for two people and consisted of a living-room with curtained-off bedroom, a small kitchen, with the usual additional offices.

Bournville Almshouses – now known as The Quadrangle.

173

According to Iolo A. Williams in his book *The Firm of Cadbury, 1831-1931*:

> Each dwelling is planned to accommodate two people – a husband and wife, or a mother and daughter – and fire, light, and medical attendance are provided free of charge. The houses are furnished with good and solid oak furniture. There is a common-room, where meetings and the like may be held.
>
> The inmates must be sixty years or more of age, and must have some small means of their own – at least ten shillings a week for a single person, or fifteen shillings for a married couple. The income of a single person, however, must not exceed a hundred, nor that of a married couple a hundred and twenty, pounds a year. Adjoining the almshouses are thirty-eight houses, the rents from which go towards the upkeep of the foundation.

Bournville Almshouses – inner courtyard.

Now referred to as 'The Quadrangle' the buildings have, in recent years, been completely modernised and now provide accommodation for 33 residents.

The majority of the 38 houses have been converted to provide flats the rents of which still provide income toward the upkeep of the Quadrangle.

The *Bournville Village Trust Annual Report* for 1984 includes the following item:

> Bournville Village Trustees also sit as Trustees of the Bournville Almshouses Trust, a separate Charity set up and endowed by Richard Cadbury in 1898. . . . The Almshouses were originally only for ex-employees of Cadbury Brothers, but more recently this eligibility has been widened to include other categories of pensioner as well. Starting in 1979, all the bungalows in The Quadrangle underwent a comprehensive programme of rehabilitation and modernisation which on its completion in 1982, provided all residents with fully up-to-date facilities in each home.

During 1986, the bungalows underwent major re-roofing work which lasted throughout most of the year. At the time it was said that:

> The Trustees remain concerned that the rental income from the endowment houses does not provide sufficient money to meet all the costs of managing and maintaining the Almshouses, and they will be looking at ways to overcome this problem in 1987.

I have read through subsequent Bournville Village Trust annual reports but to my knowledge there has been no indication as to how the shortfall was met, however, I am led to believe the cost of upkeep and maintenance of the Almshouses at the present time is covered by monies received by way of rent of the houses/flats.

Selly Oak Colleges

In 1955 there were, in the Bristol Road, Weoley Park Road area of the Estate, 11 residential institutions known as the Selly Oak Colleges. A Bournville Village Trust Publication entitled *The Bournville Village Trust 1900-1955* includes the following.

175

Each College stands in its own grounds and has its own corporate life. The Central Buildings include the George Cadbury Hall, the Library, lecture rooms, offices and common rooms. There are also playing fields nearby. The total number of students in residence varies between 200 and 300.

The Selly Oak Colleges became a definite association in 1919, when five of those already existing agreed to establish a Central Council, which is now representative also of those colleges which have since been affiliated to it.

The original five Colleges are:

WOODBROOKE, once the home of George Cadbury; established in 1903 as an educational settlement by members of the Society of Friends though residence is not limited to that body. Offers a wide range of courses for preparation for Christian service in many fields, a course in International Relations, and a Social Study Diploma Course.

KINGSMEAD, established 1905 as a training college for missionaries. Originally for men and women of the Friends' Foreign Missionary Association, from 1933 it was under a joint Committee of the Friends' Service Council and the Methodist Missionary Society. In 1952 the Friends' Service Council arranged to send their candidates for training to Woodbrooke, and the Methodist Missionary Society is therefore now solely responsible for Kingsmead.

WESTHILL, founded 1907, is the recognised College of the Free Churches for Christian Education. Trains students as voluntary or professional leaders in work for children and young people. It has courses for the Certificate in Youth Service (Birmingham University) and the Westhill Certificate in Christian Education; it also trains day school teachers – organising courses for the national Froebel Foundation, and for the Birmingham University Certificate. Westhill also has a practice school, and both College and School are recognised by the Ministry of Education.

FIRCROFT (1909): a residential college for adult male industrial and commercial employees. Its purpose is to help those who left school at 14 or 15 to develop their capacities for service to the community.

176

(The original building used by Fircroft was 'The Dell' in Oak Tree Lane, Bournville, the site of the present Head Office of Bournville Village Trust.)

In association with Fircroft is AVONCROFT (1925), a similar institution for rural workers. Originally at Offenham, near Evesham, in 1935 it was removed to Stoke Prior, near Bromsgrove. In 1952, Avoncroft began to cater for various organisations offering courses in adult education to both rural and urban students.

CAREY HALL, founded 1912, for the training of women missionaries of the Presbyterian Church of England, and the Baptist and London Missionaries Societies.

Besides Avoncroft, the following Colleges have been set up since the original association was founded.

COLLEGE OF THE ASCENSION: trains women of the Anglican communion for work in the Church at home and overseas, under the auspices of the Society for the Propagation of the Gospel. Founded 1923.

YWCA College: started work at Selly Oak in 1926, but founded in 1896. Trains YWCA leaders and youth workers for service at home and abroad.

OVERDALE COLLEGE (1920), trains ministers, missionaries and other workers for the Churches of Christ, but membership is not confined to this denomination.

ST ANDREW'S COLLEGE (1946), is for men missionaries of several denominations.

INDUSTRIAL CHRISTIAN FELLOWSHIP COLLEGE. An Anglican foundation removed to Selly Oak in 1953. Trains laymen for mission work in factories and industrial areas of large towns.

There have been many changes throughout the years, and, in answer to a recent enquiry as to how many Selly Oak Colleges there are at the present time, I was told, eight. They are, The College of the Ascension, Crowther Hall, Fircroft, Prospect Hall, Springdale, St Andrew's, Westhill and Woodbrooke.

SELLY OAK COLLEGES LIBRARY, founded in 1925 owes its foundation largely to the generosity of members of the Cadbury family.

The present building, constructed in 1932, was built primarily for the use of members of the colleges and was the gift of Mr and Mrs Edward Cadbury. In addition to a large comprehensive selection of books and periodicals on Religion and Theology, Social Sciences, Education and Oriental Studies, it also houses and administers the Mingana collection of oriental manuscripts, comprising about 600 Syriac, 1,500 Arabic and a number of Persian, Ethiopic and other documents, and the Rendel Harris collection of papyri.

In 1927 Elizabeth Cadbury funded the building of a central hall in memory of her husband and it was named 'GEORGE CADBURY HALL'. Designed by Hubert Lidbetter it was built to seat 500. At the opening ceremony Elizabeth Cadbury handed the building over to the Council of the Selly Oak Colleges and expressed the hope that it would be used for the purposes for which the Colleges existed – namely, for the study of religious and social problems, and to give opportunity to men and women to equip themselves for the service of God and their fellow man. It would also be available for recreation, for stimulating interest in art, music, literature and drama.

Bournville Village Festival

The first Bournville Village Festival was held in 1902. In 1982 the late Mrs G. Carley and Mrs Dorothy Griffin produced the following brief history of the Bournville Maypole for inclusion in the 80th anniversary programme, and I am indebted to their families for allowing me to re-produce the article in full.

In 1902, in common with the rest of the country, the small village of Bournville (then only about 400 houses) decided to celebrate the Coronation of King Edward VII by holding 'Bournville Village Coronation Festivities'. This was held on 2nd July and was the inspiration of what is now 'Bournville Village Festival'. The programme on the day started with a procession of lorries around the village; each had a different theme representing the British Isles, May Queen and her attendants, Maypole Dancers, and Sylvan Scene. There followed a varied pattern, very much after the style we know now – Maypole, Sports, Tug-o-war, Morris Dancers. Tea for the children: the finale, at 8.30 p.m., was *Sir Roger de Coverley* by the whole of the residents. One item was *Madrigal Party on the Lake*;

Programme for the first ever Bournville Village Festival 1902 – forerunner of Bournville Children's Festival.

this was on Martin's Pool, a very pretty lake where the car park next to Linden Road Baths now stands.

The first Festival was so greatly enjoyed that it was decided to make it an annual event with the Maypole as the centrepiece, and from early April, several times a week, practices were held at the children's playground in Laurel Grove. The original Festival Committee was formed into the Bournville Village Council in 1903 and, since that time, has organised the Festival as well as being the local Residents' Association.

In 1906 a play *The Queen of Storyland* was written by Mrs F. Cottrell, a local resident, and was performed as part of the festivities. The characters were mainly nursery rhyme figures. Also on this occasion there was a fancy dress parade of adults as well as children, swimming, sports, and a polo team: the finale was *A Lantern Maze*.

Then came the First World War, and these activities came to a halt. In 1919 however, a Peace Celebration Festival was held.

Maypole dancers, 1902?

Fancy dress competitors, 1919.

Children and staff from the school joined in, dressed as story book and nursery rhyme characters, to attend 'The Lord Mayor's Ball'. The plays were held in the Girls' Recreation Grounds, everyone trooping across Bournville Lane by way of the wooden bridge after tea. An important part of the event was the tea provided for the village children; mothers and school staff were busy cutting and buttering bread all morning to have everything ready in time. In the days before the Cadbury Dining Block was built, the children's tea was served under the verandah at the Girls' Pavilion (now Bournville Club).

The Maypole was repeated in some years when the Village Flower Show was held in the Park (then owned by Bournville Village Trust) and the schools. If one looks carefully a gate can still be seen in the boundary railings near the new Infant School building; this was opened so that visitors could pass easily from the schools into the park.

The Maypole continued without a break until 1939 when, once again, war put a stop to it. Interest and continuity in the Maypole, however, were fostered by performances at Rowheath as part of the 'Holidays at Home' scheme organised by the City. After the war the Festival came to life once more. This was a time of many difficulties, but a band of enthusiastic helpers overcame obstacles galore. The sideshows came out of store and new ones were devised. Only the Men's Recreation Grounds were used but, again, the Maypole was a major attraction. Now about 120 girls take part – the Festival Queen and ribbon girls are always Bournville residents, but extra dancers are drawn from a wider area if the need arises.

A variety of different attractions have appeared over the years – bellringers, trampoline displays, a mini circus, fire-brigade displays, police dogs, the list is endless.

In 1977 the Jubilee Festival celebrated the 75th anniversary. Although the content has changed over the years (this is necessary to maintain the life of the Festival), the Maypole remains the important central item, and our thanks should go to the many people who, over the years, have encouraged and trained the many numbers of dancers who have taken part in this annual event.

In 1902 the finale was *Sir Roger de Coverley*; now, in 1982, it is a spectacular firework display. Times and interests have changed but the spirit of the Festival as a 'village' celebration continues whilst at the same time giving pleasure to folk from far and wide.

> Happy Bournville, home of delight,
> Praise it we will, with all our might.

(Quoted from the 1902 Festival programme.)

I am fortunate in having an original programme of events from the 1902 Festival among my treasured possessions. It gives details of the procession through the village which read thus;

> A Procession, headed by the Bournville Brass Band, will start from Maryvale Road and parade the Village by way of Linden Road, Bournville Lane, Row Heath Lane, Maryvale Road, Linden Road, Sycamore Road, Willow Road, Raddle Barn Lane, Elm Road, Laburnum Road, Triangle, Willow Road, Acacia Road, Linden Road to Bournville Lane, and will enter the Recreation Grounds by Bournville Lane, arriving about 2.00 p.m. Each child must present a Ticket upon entering.

List of Characters in Fancy Dress.
(To be included in the procession)

1st Lorry	Representative of the British Isles.
2nd Lorry	Illustrative of Greater Britain.
3rd Lorry	May Queen and her attendants.
4th Lorry	May Pole dancers.
5th Lorry	Sylvan Scene.

Red Riding Hood	Bo-Peeps
Little Boy Blue	Milk Maids
Flower Girls	Midshipman
Clowns	Japanese
Italians	Robin Hood
Shepherds	Shepherdess
Mary and her lamb	John Bull
Peace	Nurses
Ambulance	King's Herald

182

*My father with Mrs G. Carley who for many years trained the Maypole
dancers.*

Morris Dancers, Cricketers, etc., etc.

Ten little nigger boys.

At intervals during the afternoon the Bournville Brass Band
will play selections of music.

ORDER OF THE DAY

11.30	Children meet in the field near the station, Mary Vale Road.
12 till 2	Procession
2 till 2.30	Children assemble
2.30 to 3.30	May-Pole dance and crowning of the May Queen Plantation songs
3.30 to 3.45	Morris dancers
3.45 to 4	Boys' Tug-of-war
4 to 5	Children's tea

MUSIC BY THE BAND

5 till 6	Adults' tea
6 to 7	Sports
7 to 8	Comic Cricket Match
8 to 8.30	Madrigal party on the Lake
8.30 to 8.50	Sir Roger De Coverley
	(by the whole of the residents)
9.00	National Anthem by the Band and Children

SPORTS 6 to 7		Prize –	1st	2nd	3rd
Sack Race	Boys under 14		5/-	3/-	2/-
Egg and Spoon Race	Girls under 14		5/-	3/-	2/-
Needle-threading Race	Ladies		5/-	3/-	2/-
Lighted Candle Race	Men		5/-	3/-	2/-

Tug-of-War, for boys under 16 years – eight in a team

1st Heat

North side	Prizes,	8 caps	
Elm Road		v	Willow Road
Raddle Barn Lane		v	Laburnum Road

1st Heat

South side	Prizes,	8 caps	
Beech Road		v	Bournville Lane
Mary Vale Road		v	Linden Road

To be pulled in heats; one pull to decide the first heats.
The best of three pulls to decide the final.
Entries to be made for Sports not later than June 25th
to the Hon. Secretaries

PROGRAMME OF MUSIC
by the Band

Conductor   Mr J. Loughton

Coronation March ....

The Magnet .... Pope

Violetta .... H. Round

String of Pearls .... H. Round

Darkies' Frolic .... S. Cope

Prima Donna .... H. Round

PROGRAMME PART-SONGS

Conductor   Mr Lees

Softly falls the shades of evening .... Hatton

Now pray we for our Country .... Eliza Flower

Empire's Flag .... A. C. Mackenzie

Hurrah for Merry England .... Berger

GROUNDS OPEN AT 1 o'clock

The Committee request the co-operation of the Residents
in keeping the Sports' Ground clear

Mr Compton, of Stirchley, has been appointed Official
Photographer for the occasion, who will be pleased to
supply copies of the various Groups, Tableux, etc.

Hon. Secs.: E. Wakeman, 27 Laburnum Road
T. B. Clissold, Mary Vale Road

By 1906 the programme was very similar to that of 1902 with the
addition of a Fancy Dress Parade and a Children's Play, as mentioned
in the historical account written by Mrs Carley and Mrs Griffin. The
number of races was increased by the inclusion of a 75 yards three-
legged race for boys, 50 yards potato race for girls, 75 yards flat race
for boys under 12, 75 yards flat race for boys 12–15, 75 yards skipping
race for girls, and swimming sports; 2 lengths handicap (up to 18),
Team race, and a Polo match.

During the late 50's and early 60's, my father served as Chairman
of Bournville Village Council, members of which you will remember
have been responsible for the arranging of the Children's Festival since
1903, and I have a copy of the Statement of Receipts and Payments for
Bournville Village Festival 1968 which makes interesting reading if
only in being able to compare the items of income and expenditure
with present day costs. In 1968

Money taken at the gates amounted to £248

Sale of programmes .... £ 68

Sideshows £315

Catering .... £ 95

Pop Stall .... £ 89

Hot dogs .... £ 29

Roundabouts .... £ 10
Ice Cream .... £ 18
Ponies .... £ 10
Advertisements .... £ 55
Donations .... £ 62

Total £999

Expenditure for the same year was as follows:

Fireworks £154
Printing £112
Minerals and Crisps .... £ 82
Loudspeaker system .... £ 35
Maypole expenses .... £ 22
Signboard .... £ 12
Catering £164
Gatemen, groundsmen, cleaners .... £ 25
Children's Fancy Dress prizes .... £ 11
Bournville Village Trust .... £ 30
Hot Dogs .... £ 9
Sideshows, expenses and prizes £110
Bouquets .... £ 6
Insurance .... £ 4
Entertainments .... £ 98
Surplus £126

I understand the figures for 1993 were:

Income £9,000
Expenditure £6,000
Surplus £3,000

The figure of £3,000 surplus was donated to various local charities.

As has been said many times before, those who bring sunshine into the lives of others cannot keep it from themselves, and I hope all who give their precious time and expertise to make Bournville Village Festival the success it is will always know their efforts will not be in vain.

[Excerpt from Vol. XLI., No. 3 (1921) of the Journal of The Royal Sanitary Institute.]

Teaching of Sex Hygiene.

FROM A WORKING MOTHER'S POINT OF VIEW.

By Mrs C. Guest (Birmingham).

THE importance of such teaching at the present time is clearly realised by every social worker. One has only to read the daily papers, with their sad cases of matrimonial troubles, etc., to feel that something must be done to check the evils around us. The boy and girl marriages, entered into without any thought as to the responsibilities of marriage, the open immorality, and the increasing number of cases of venereal disease, bring before us the question, 'Where have we failed?' Is it not answered in the fact that no sex-teaching has been given in the past? Boys and girls were allowed to grow up and develop without any training at all in what should be of the most importance – their responsibilities as the future parents of the race. Hence the result: can one wonder? And so to-day we are considering what is to be done to remedy things and most people advocate the teaching of sex-hygiene but are not quite clear as to the best method of teaching it. Shall it be taught by teachers who are specially trained in this subject? or shall it be taught in school by the ordinary schoolteacher? or, in the Home by the parents or guardians? While it may be a good thing to have a specially trained teacher for boys and girls whose training at home has been neglected, my objection to it generally is on the ground that the teaching is begun too late – the adolescent age has enough vital problems of its own, without that. There should be a good strong foundation laid in sex-teaching before that age. The ordinary school teacher can be of great assistance by the use of nature lessons, etc., but the first lessons, in my opinion, should be given by the mother in the home. She has every advantage in her favour – she has sole control for the first five years of a child's life, and at that time the most lasting impressions are made. Some mothers of the working class raise difficulties – they say they are not educated enough or that they have no time in their busy lives, there is enough to do in keeping the home and children clean and getting meals. Quite true! there is enough to do and far too much sometimes, but there is always time to answer a child's question, isn't there? And a child's education is partly gained by questions and answers. To the other objection, that of not being sufficiently educated, all that is needed is a little common-sense and tact, one does not talk to a child in big words but in simple language. Many mothers are beginning to see this point of view and to realise that the best results are obtainable if training is begun early. Educational experts are adopting this theory by advocating the system of nursery schools.

I suggest some methods which may be helpful to young mothers who desire to train their children in a right way. Begin in the cradle days by not letting your baby have everything it cries for: that way means a spoilt child. Then when you teach it cleanliness, try to impress upon the child's mind the fact that the body is a wonderful piece of mechanism, fashioned so that every part has its own work to do, and that we must see to it that through no neglect or ill-treatment on our part, it shall get useless. You will not be able to do this all at once, but gradually, as the child develops, this lesson of respect and care for the body as the temple of the soul can be taught. When you take your children out in the fresh air, you can tell them of the flowers and insects and birds, of the father and mother bird, making a cosy nest and then of the eggs laid in it by the mother and kept warm by her body, until hatched out and then of the busy time for both birds to feed them, until the baby birds can look after themselves. Most children have pets of their own and it is a very good thing too, because so much is learnt that way. From these nature lessons it is but a small step to that of the baby in the home and there is no nicer way of telling a child, who asks 'where baby came from,' that it came from a seed, which mother kept warm in her body until it was big enough to be born, just the same as the seeds in the garden were kept warm in the earth until big enough to come out and grow in the sunshine and the rain. This also explains to the child the reason of mother's great love, because the child is part of herself. All these lessons can be given in the ordinary every-day life of a mother and her children, boys and girls alike: no guide is needed by the child's own questions, and a mother's own sense will tell her how and when to give any information. In fact, no hard and fast rule can be laid down, so much depends on a child's development. To any who may object to this method of teaching, thinking it may lead to chatter among other children, I would say that my experience tells me that when a child is told the truth about anything, he or she does not bother about it any more – it is only when things are hushed up and made mysterious that a child's curiosity is aroused and questions are asked of anybody and everybody.

A little girl I knew, had a pair of bantams and was heard to say to the hen, just about to lay an egg, 'Never mind, henny, you'll soon be better,' and another child I knew, when told that her pussy would soon have some kittens, busied herself making a nice bed in the cupboard for them and was so careful not to hurt poor pussy. This shows that a spirit of love and care for others is being taught to the children, which is never forgotten by them. But one thing which perhaps will have more weight in combating any objections is the fact that a child has to gain this knowledge sometime, and children, who are of the poorer classes, have to go to schools where there are large classes and where it is impossible for any teacher to know everything that is going on, and we know that much undesirable talk goes on at times. Is it not infinitely more desirable that sex-knowledge shall be given in a nice clean way to the child at home, than for it to pick up any rubbish outside? So much for the childish days, but the time goes on and the child nears the adolescent age, with all its changes. Are you going to take the child on one side and tell him or her what it means? It is a parent's bounden duty to do so at that time, even if instruction of some kind has not been given previously. It is just at the time of change from childhood to young men and women that the most help is needed. And if there is a strong bond of love between parent and child, if a child reposes all confidence in the parents, then, naturally, will the child, either boy or girl seek advice from its parents. Naturally and quite easily, too, will the mother, or father maybe, explain the changes taking place, tell of the responsibilities in connection with them, and warn of probable temptations. The adolescent can be told of the need to keep a clean, healthy body, in readiness for the time coming on when marriage is desired, the harm that is done to the children of the future if an unhealthy life is led. Need one say more except that to urge every young mother, who earnestly desires the welfare of her child, to commence this training early. Teach a love of truth, care for the weaker ones, self-control, cleanliness and a high standard of its responsibilities as future parents of the race. Establish a mutual bond of love and confidence between you and the child, and, doing this, you need not fear the time to come when the child has to stand alone. It seems to me that if every mother shouldered her task, in this way, within the next few years, a great change would be apparent. Everyone realises the need for something to be done; shall we women, mothers in the home, do that part which lies nearest to us? It may not seem much, perhaps, just to train one or two young lives in the right way: how much, it *really* means can only be realised after many years, when the children, so trained, have passed on the training to their offspring and a cleaner, healthier, happier race is the result.

Memories of Bournville School 1908-1915

(Being a copy of a talk given by Marian C. Owen to the Parent/ Teachers Association on the occasion of the School's Diamond Jubilee in 1966.)

During the year 1908 when I was a little over infant age my parents came to live in a new house on the Bournville Estate and overlooking the Park. At the time of the move I was in hospital recovering from scarlet fever and was unable to begin school until almost the end of the year. I shall always remember my first visit to the school, everything about it looked new, although, it had already been in existence for over two years and in every way it seemed different from the school I had previously attended. From the time of entering as a junior, until the time came for me to leave in 1915, was undoubtedly, a most happy period of my life and I would like, very briefly, to share with you some memories of the first years of the life of the school.

The classes in those days, as far as I can remember, were not mixed and it was only at Morning Assembly and on special occasions that we came into contact with the boys. Mr James Fielden was Headmaster of the School and Mrs Ella Brown Headmistress of the Girls' Department. She was held in great awe by all the girls and it was only when we reached the Seventh Standard, of which she was in charge, that we realised she was human after all and a very wise, kind and understanding person.

Among the staff there were two who continued at the school until retirement, years after I had left, namely Mr E. J. Horsley and Mr A. G. Barker. Miss Esme Jones too, taught at the school during those early years until her marriage to Mr Horsley.

As recently as two years ago I had the pleasure of renewing friendship with Miss M. E. Evans, now Mrs Pugh and living at Colwyn Bay, who was a teacher at the school from 1909 until her marriage in 1930. During her visit to Bournville last autumn Mr Lewis (the now headmaster), kindly allowed us to call on him at the school and we were both very impressed with alterations and extensions to the school buildings.

My most vivid impressions of those early days were of the laundry and cookery departments situated in the basement. I feel sure that there must have been times when I took articles other than a stiff white collar to be laundered but I can only recall the special treatment meted out to this particular one and at which somewhere along the line gum arabic was used. Not once did I hear my father complain at having to wear the said collar. Perhaps it never was worn again but only put aside for me to take to school from time to time.

The cookery room was well equipped with cupboards, well scrubbed tables and what seemed to me at the time, an enormous gas-cooker, known in those days as a stove. There was also seating accommodation and after the practical work and whilst the cooking was in progress the girls would seat themselves on the pew-like forms which were arranged in tiers and the mistress would continue her lesson.

For many years a Sunday School was held in the Junior and Infant Schools and the Senior group met in the cookery room. I well remember going early to help prepare the room and having to place a green tablecloth over the gas cooker on which were laid the Bible, a hymn book and a vase of flowers.

Alas, laundry and cookery and baby-care departments have, with senior scholars, moved away to other schools, and only memories remain. I am sure it would surprise many people today to hear that Bournville School even at that time had a baby-care class which had the responsibility of taking sole charge from 10 a.m. to 4 p.m. of a very young baby. The pupils would be taught how to bathe the baby, prepare and give it its bottle and would wash the daily dozen. This, remember, was at a time when there were no day nurseries and mothers stayed at home to look after their babies.

Leaving the basement one re-entered the school through the girls' entrance near to which was a staircase leading to the library. What a wonderful library it was too in those far off days, where silence as you entered was spontaneous and one crept

191

quietly around the bookshelves, searching for a book of one's choice and, having chosen, would take it to one of the large oak tables and seat oneself in a beautiful leather-padded chair for an undisturbed hour of reading. How very fortunate we were to have a school curriculum which included one session per week in such a lovely well-equipped library.

Continuing up the stairs would bring us to the Art room, a veritable paradise for budding artists, and with such wonderful views from its windows. For those not interested in art, there was always the fascination of stealing a glance at the mechanism of the school clock which was housed at the other side of a glass partition. In our musings we were quickly brought back to earth by the boom of the clock chiming every fifteen minutes. Outside the Art-room a spiral staircase led to the tower, but children were not allowed to climb it until their last day at school, when they would be given the opportunity of inspecting the bells in the tower and also of viewing the countryside for miles around.

The Schools,
Bournville
Jan. 16th 1915.

During the time Marion-Guest has attended Bournville School she has given the greatest satisfaction as a pupil. She has passed successfully through the various standards and is now working in Std. Gr. y. Her work has invariably been done in the most conscientious manner and her progress has been most creditable.

She has shown intelligence above the average in "English" subjects e.g. Grammar, Reading, Recitation, Spelling and Dictation. She bears an excellent character for obedience, diligence, and honourable conduct generally.

Ellen B. Brown.
(Chief Mistress.)

If further information is required please refer to :-
Mrs. E. B. Brown,
The Schools,
Bournville

During this spectacular period in the life of the school, the children were quite used to having visitors who were usually accompanied by George Cadbury and his wife Elizabeth, who later became Dame Elizabeth Cadbury. The visitors came from all over the world, mainly to see for themselves the model village of Bournville. Among them were a party of Germans, who, after hearing a class of children singing, in turn sang to them. Little did we realise that two years later our countries would be at war with each other.

Other events which I remember quite clearly include a visit to the zoo in London where I had my first ride on an elephant, and I re-call how Miss Hilda Pumphrey, Headmistress of the Infants' School, a lady of ample proportions, walked around feeding the animals with biscuits which she carried in a huge alpaca bag fastened round her waist. When the younger children fell asleep on the journey home by train, she soon deposited them on the luggage racks where they remained until Bournville station was reached.

City of Birmingham Education Committee.

Bournville _____ School.
Mixed _____ Department.
Dec. 11th 1914

Report of Marion Guest.

Geography	Ex.
History	V.G.
Science	V.G.
Composition	Ex.
Reading	Ex.
Recitation	Ex.
Spelling	Ex.
Hand Writing	V.G.
Grammar.	Ex.
Arithmetic	V.G.
Drawing	G.
Music	Ex.
Needlework.	Ex.

Marion's work has been highly satisfactory so much so that she has gained the distinction of winning the prize for general proficiency in Std. y. for 1914.

Ellen B Brown.
(Chief Mistress
Bournville School)

The Staff – Bournville Infant School.
Back row: Miss Showell, Miss Pumphrey, Miss Latter.
Front row: Miss Whitehouse, Miss Woodall.

The weddings, at the Friends' Meeting House, of the daughters of Mr George Cadbury by his first marriage were, indeed, red letter days for the school children and on both occasions they, suitably dressed in their Sunday best, gathered in front of the Ruskin Hall and sang as the bridal couple emerged from the Meeting House and specially chosen children scattered rose petals as they made their way down the path.

Annual events were the Christmas party and Children's Festival. I still have in my possession an invitation which reads:

> The Misses and Masters Cadbury invite
> bearer to Christmas party at the Schools
> Bournville at 5 p.m. Friday evening
> December 18th 1908.

On Christmas party days the hall always looked cheerful with a Christmas tree and holly decorations. The girls would don their party dresses with gaily coloured sashes and the boys wore their best suits. Trestle tables, covered with white tablecloths reaching

194

down to the floor, would be heavily laden with a sumptuous tea. After tea an entertainment was given which usually included a moving picture show, always most fascinating to watch as at the time there were no local Picture Houses. The party would end with the singing of carols and, as we filed out of the hall, excited and happy, we would receive a gift of a novelty box of chocolates, an apple and an orange from Father Christmas.

My mother as a 'Prince in Disguise', 1914.

With other members of the cast.

195

Party invitations - 1908 and 1909.

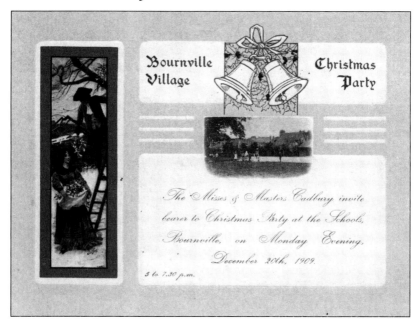

Festival Tea – Girls' Pavilion, 1922.
Mr Wakeman – Chairman Bournville Village Council in conversation
with Mr James Fielden – Headmaster.

We all looked forward to Spring for it would be during that time that one or two members of the Children's Festival Committee (most of the parents helped in one way or another at this annual event), would call at the school to find out who wished to take part in the Maypole dances and/or perform in a play. Auditions were held and to this day I remember standing on the platform in the hall and reciting a poem entitled *The Sea*. This evidently impressed the judges, for I was chosen to take the part of a Queen named Goldilocks. Alas! disappointment awaited me the following day, the judges having omitted to take the name of the Queen into consideration were very sorry, etc., etc., but they would have to try to find someone with golden hair, mine was known as mouse-coloured. It was through my mother that they eventually found someone, who do you think? The girl who lived next door!!! My disappointment, however, turned to happiness the following year for I was chosen to take the part of a Prince in Disguise and my greatest thrill was when the Principals were taken to Astleys of Broad Street for their theatrical costumes. This, I believe, was the only time that the committee responsible for the production of the Festival play decided to hire outfits. That was in 1914 and the last Festival to be held until after the war, which began in August of that year, had ended.

It was with a sorrowful heart, in late January 1915, that I said my 'good-byes' to the school. A very happy period of my life had come to an end.

The cost of setting up home in 1924 – my parents' bills.

HOUSEHOLD GOODS PURCHASED FROM
TEN ACRES AND STIRCHLEY CO-OPERATIVE SOCIETY

Bedding Department

Miss Guest, 4a Selly Oak Road, Bournville

May 1924		£	s	d
2 pairs blankets	@ 35/–d	3	10	0
2 blankets cotton	@ 4/6d each		9	0
1 bed-spread	@ 15/11d each		15	11
18 yards sheeting	@ 2/11½d per yard	2	13	3
2 yards calico	@ 1/6½d per yard		3	1
25½ yards casement curtaining @ 1/4½d per yard		1	15	1
6 yards roller towelling @ 1/3d per yard			7	6
Total		9	13	10

Furnishing Department

Miss Guest, 4a Selly Oak Road, Bournville

6.6.1924	£	s	d
Bucket		1	6
Hair broom, complete		4	1
Hand brush		2	6
Shovel			7½
Scrubbing brush			8½

198

	£	s	d
9 yards Oilcloth @ 4/3d per yard	1	18	3
8½ yards Linoleum @ 7/3d per yard	3	1	9
3 x 2½ yard tapestry square	2	13	6
Rug		12	9
2 reversible rugs @ 13/9d each	1	7	6
Wool mattress	1	19	6
Bolster set	1	3	6
Mattress pad		5	6
Bedroom chair		8	6
2 No. 1 Coconut mats @ 2/6d		5	0
Clothes basket		2	6
No. 1 cast kettle		7	9
Enamel colander		1	5½
Enamel bowls @ 2/2d and 1/10½d		4	0½
Coco broom, complete		1	7
Coal hod		3	9
Clothes line		1	2
Pegs			6
Window leather		2	0
Hearth plate 2/4d, dredger 6d		2	10
6 plates 2/6, dish 7½d		3	1½
Jugs (2)		1	8½
Total	**15**	**17**	**7**

In addition to the above items for which I have the original receipts, I also have a hand-written account for the following:

Mr E. Owen, 46 Raddlebarn Road

27.5.1924	£	s	d
Front room suite	12	15	0
Bedroom suite	18	0	0
Bedsteads	3	10	0
4 small chairs @ 9/6d each	1	18	0
2 reclining chairs @ 28/6d each	2	17	0
Table	5	0	0
Total	**44**	**0**	**0**

From the above figures it would appear my parents furnished their first home for about £70.

I am reliably informed a comparable figure for today would be in the region of £7,000.

Testimonials

From Mr W. R. P. Steward, Building Surveyor, 1 Acacia Road.

25th August 1930.

To whom it may concern.

Mr E. Owen of 8 Selly Oak Road, Bournville, worked in the Bournville Trust Building Department under my supervision for approximately four years. He served chiefly as motor driver with responsibility for overhaul and ordinary repairs on a Morris 1 ton truck.

From my personal experience I can recommend him as an industrious worker who considered the interests of the Department thoroughly. He is an honest, sober man and an excellent timekeeper. I shall be pleased to satisfy a prospective employer on any particular point desired.

Signed W. R. P. Steward.

From Leonard P. Appleton, Secretary and Manager Bournville Village Trust.

25th August 1930.

To whom it may concern.

Edgar Owen who was employed by the Bournville Village Trust for seven and half years from 1920, left because the department was closed. He was first employed as a gardener, and afterwards as a motor driver, and for nine months he was in charge of the low-pressure boiler at the Day Continuation School.

During the whole time he was employed by the Trust he gave every satisfaction, being an industrious, willing and honest worker.

Signed Leonard P. Appleton.

Secretary and Manager.

Copies of Letters my Father received when he retired in 1963

It is with very great regret that we heard from you yesterday that you feel you must give up the work which you have been doing for so long as gardening contractor to the Trust. I should like you to know how much we have appreciated your work, and especially the close interest which you have taken in the development of the newer areas of the Estate and in the Estate as a whole.

Although I know that you have been glad to do it, I would like to say here how much too we have valued your work as Chairman of the Village Council and the service which you have given on other Committees, such as the School Managers and the Council of Churches.

I shall certainly report your proposed retirement to the Trustees and I expect I shall be writing to you again.

With regard to the specific point concerning your plant and equipment, I confirm that we shall be glad to purchase this, and perhaps you would kindly let me have a list of what you have for sale.

I should like to add that personally I very much regret that this decision has become necessary, and to let you know how very much I have valued all that you have done and your constant readiness to help.

With best wishes to you and Mrs Owen.

Yours sincerely,

F. Ralph Barlow.

21st January

It was reported to our Trustees' Meeting last week that you will be giving up your work as landscape gardening contractor. It was noted that you had done practically all landscaping in the Shenley area and on other parts of the Estate since building was resumed after the War, and the Trustees have asked me to write and say how much they have valued the work which you have done and the interest which you have always shown in the development of the Estate.

I am also glad to take this opportunity of letting you know that the Trustees greatly appreciate what you have done as Chairman of the

201

Bournville Village Council. They realise how much the life of the Estate owes to you and those who have served with you on the Council. They are also very sensible of the service which you have given as a member of the School Managers Committee, the Ruskin Hall Committee and of the Bournville Council of Churches.

In recognition of all that you have done they have asked me to send you the enclosed cheque as a token of their appreciation. I should like to send you and Mrs Owen my very best wishes for the future.

Yours sincerely

L. J. Cadbury, Chairman.

Bournville Village Trustees.

Bibliography

LIFE OF GEORGE CADBURY, by A. G. Gardiner, published by Cassell. 1923.

THE FIRM OF CADBURY, by Iolo A. Williams, published by Constable and Co. 1931.

ELIZABETH CADBURY 1858-1951, published by George G. Harrap and Co. Ltd. 1955.

BOURNVILLE JUNIOR SCHOOL, THE FIRST EIGHTY YEARS, 1906-1986, by Mr Andrew Macfarlane. 1986.

BOURNVILLE COLLEGE OF FURTHER EDUCATION, 75 YEARS OF CONTINUITY AND CHANGE 1913-1988, by Albert Weedall, OBE, David J. Ward and Patricia M. Twyman.

SELLY OAK COLLEGES, GLIMPSES OF THE FIRST 70 YEARS, by Rev. David E. Mole. 1994.

Sundry booklets published either by Cadbury Bournville, Bournville Village Council or Bournville Village Trust, from 1895 to present day.